I0820173

TRUST YOUR GUT

one of these delicious
or make your own!
Açai
Nutty Cocoa
Bowl
Acai Puree
Banana
Cocoa Powder
Açai
America
Fashion Bowl
Acai Puree
Açaí is

TRUST YOUR GUT

ANTI-INFLAMMATORY RECIPES FOR FEELING UNSTOPPABLE

JENNIFER FISHER

THIS BOOK IS DEDICATED TO MY FATHER, PAPA JOHN.
THE MAN, THE MYTH, AND THE LEGEND
WHO WILL FOREVER REMAIN IN THE HEARTS
OF ALL OF US WHO KNEW HIM
(OR WHO GOT TO SEE HIM IN ACTION ON MY INSTAGRAM AND IRL).
HE TAUGHT ME HOW TO COOK WITH FIRE
(LITERALLY AND FIGURATIVELY),
HOW TO FORAGE FOR FRESH VEGETABLES
(FROM OTHERS' YARDS OR OUR OWN OR THE SIDE OF THE ROAD, LOL),
AND MOST IMPORTANTLY TO NOT GIVE A FUCK
WHAT OTHERS THINK AND TO ALWAYS BE MYSELF.

AND TO MY MOTHER, LAUREN,
THE GENTLE FORCE WHO TAUGHT ME YOU ONLY GET ONE CHANCE
TO MAKE A FIRST IMPRESSION, SO JUST GO FOR IT,
TAKE ON ANY "ADVENTURE" THAT LIFE THROWS YOUR WAY,
OR YOU'LL NEVER KNOW—AND WHAT A SHAME IT WOULD BE TO MISS
OUT ON THAT OPPORTUNITY. THANK YOU FOR GIVING ME THE STRENGTH
TO ALWAYS BELIEVE IN MYSELF.

SO HERE I AM. GOING FOR IT . . .
THX, MOM AND DAD, FOR GIVING ME NOT ONLY THE SELF-MOTIVATION,
GRIT, AND DETERMINATION TO GET OUT THERE AND BE
A SELF-STARTER, BUT ALSO THE PERSONAL STRENGTH
AND BELIEF IN MYSELF TO KEEP GOING IF I FAIL AND
THE DETERMINATION TO GET STRONGER AND SMARTER ALONG THE WAY.

XO, SCOOTER
(YUP, THAT'S THE FAMILY NICKNAME MY FATHER GAVE ME WHEN I WAS
YOUNG BECAUSE I NEVER STOP; I JUST KEEP "SCOOTING.")

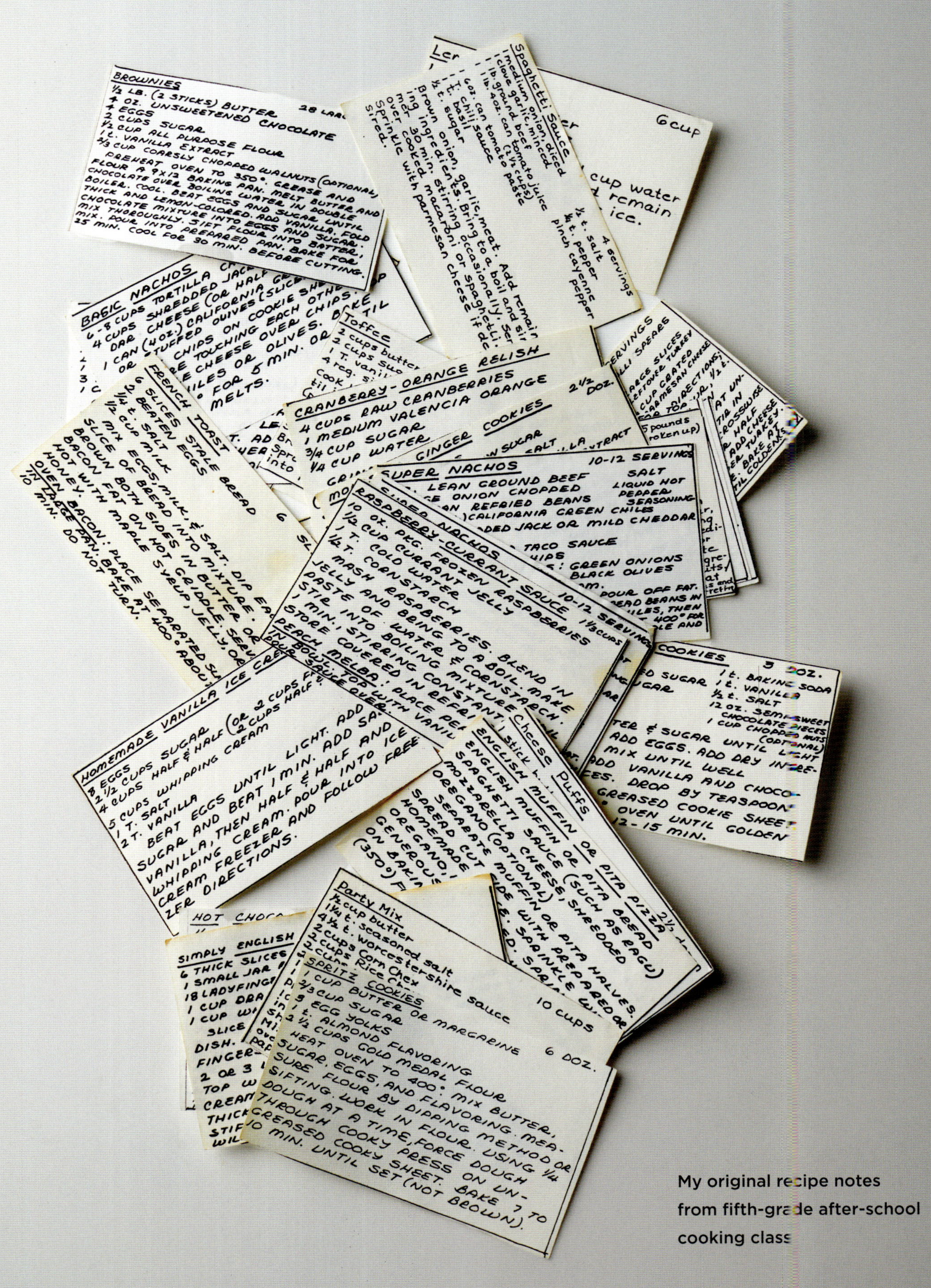

My original recipe notes from fifth-grade after-school cooking class

CONTENTS

PUEBCO INC. PL-49

FOREWORD

BY DR. WILL COLE

Having started the first functional medicine telehealth center in the world many years ago, I've had the privilege of guiding thousands of telehealth patients around the world on their journey to wellness. Few have inspired me as much as Jennifer Fisher, who came to me seeking a path forward from her health struggles. Through our work together, I witnessed a remarkable transformation—of body, mind, and philosophy—that I'm honored and excited to see elaborated upon in the pages of this book.

As a telehealth patient, Jennifer is a shining example of what it means to regain vibrant wellness. With a willingness to learn, a commitment to self-care, and an appetite for understanding the complexity of health in the modern day, she embarked on a journey of discovery, exploring the world of nutrition and ingredients. And what she found was nothing short of remarkable. As she began to make conscious choices about the foods she ingested, her body and mind underwent a profound transformation. The elimination of dairy, grains, and legumes was a game-changer, and she soon found herself feeling more energized, more focused, and more alive than she had in years.

This book is not just a collection of recipes (although for those there are plenty); it's a road map for those seeking to make positive changes in their lives through the wonderful love language of food. With Jennifer's signature warmth and generosity, these pages guide readers through the process of stocking their pantries, preparing delicious and anti-inflammatory meals, and making informed choices at the grocery store.

I can attest to the recipes' simplicity, flavor, and nutritional value. From "clean Joes" to grain-free pasta bakes, these dishes are the makings of household staples for years to come. They are neither restrictive nor deprivation-based; they're simply the building blocks for delicious, wholesome food that will make you feel amazing.

The basis of my own work is studying and putting into practice the impact food can have on our health. Our body is alive because of brilliant biochemistry, and the foods we eat dynamically influence every single cell of our body. Jennifer's approach to food is not about rules; it's about empowerment, education, and simple shifts that make healthy eating intuitive and a source of joy. By arming yourself with the right knowledge and tools, you can use the guidance throughout this book to begin taking control of your own health for the long haul.

What I appreciate most about the approach laid out in these chapters is Jennifer's willingness to share her knowledge without pretension. She's not a self-proclaimed expert or guru; she's simply a good friend who's been on a similar journey and wants to help others along the way. With a refreshing lack of ego and a generous spirit, these pages offer guidance and support, rather than dictates or dogma. Her message is clear: Taking control of your health and wellness is within reach, and she's here to help you get started.

I'm so grateful to have been a part of Jennifer's journey, and I'm thrilled to recommend this book to anyone seeking to make positive changes in their life. With these pages as a guide, you'll be well on your way to nourishing your body and mind, and living the vibrant, healthy life you deserve.

BUTTER /
SPREAD
GOYA
tostones
CHIPS
ORIGINAL
Wolff's

INTRODUCTION

This book serves up hard-won lessons on how to eat to feel my best, and I hope there is a lot here that can help you start or continue your own journey to feeling and looking better. Maybe you are tired (I used to be exhausted most of my waking life). Maybe you feel bloated. Maybe you are struggling with thinking clearly or feel hot and puffy a lot, or just feel sort of . . . off. You kind of live with it, think it's probably just age or you are too busy or it is because you have young kids or a crazy job or just have never been a great sleeper. I was this way too. But now I am not. And that is why I wanted to do this book.

ON TRUSTING YOUR GUT

This book and the 100-plus recipes are for *all* of us who just want to feel better. Say goodbye to the trendy bullshit diets, stop with your cleanses, and quit your smoothies, because this is not a diet. This is about learning to truly listen to yourself to help you make the right choices for yourself and your health, both body and mind.

I wasted years of my life bloated and fatigued, endlessly searching for the magic pill, powder, or bar that was going to put an end to my perpetual sleeplessness, grumpiness, and full-body swelling. I went to every trendy nutritionist in LA and NYC, only to be rewarded with massive bills for yet another lab test and still more supplements to add to my collection. Again and again I'd come out feeling the same as I did before the treatments, or I'd develop "fun" side effects from being pumped full of supplements and potions. Having lived with a chronic thyroid disease (Hashimoto's thyroiditis, to be exact) for most of my adult life, I resigned myself to my puffiness and forgetfulness. I figured "it is what it is" and that I just had to live with it. Little did I know I was simply eating the incorrect foods and nourishing myself with the wrong ingredients.

I started feeling off when I was a teenager, a time in my life that was super fun when it came to my health and wellness. I had cystic acne, irregular periods, and mood swings, and I was treated for the one thing doctors could see: my skin. I was a frequent flier at the dermatologist for one issue or another. The answer was always some antibiotic or adjustment to my birth control pill as a fix to whatever was going on with me. What I ate was never addressed by any of the doctors I saw. Food, including the ingredients found in packaged foods, wasn't actively addressed by the medical community back then, outside of the diet culture, and that was an industry entirely focused on weight loss. Again, treating the thing that the world could see: the external inflammation, the symptom.

However, being from Santa Barbara, California, I have always been drawn to a healthier lifestyle. Montecito in the eighties and nineties was one of Southern California's crunchier, health-focused beach towns. In high school my friends and I would toss back wheatgrass shots on weekends at the health food store downtown and tote our dense, grainy, fruity muffins (so heavy they could sub for a weapon if needed) to the beach with our sugar-laden so-called sorbet smoothies. These snacks seemed healthy at the time, but looking back, I see that we were chugging and chowing down on cane sugar, gluten, and seed oils without even realizing it. That said, it was healthier than the desserts from the Wonder Bread outlet in Santa Barbara that my parents used to buy for us—our favorite wax chocolate–coated doughnut packs and the lard-fried apple fruit pies we would beg for as dessert. We just didn't know any better. I grew up eating fruit cocktail from the can (the cherries and pears were my favorite chunks) and American cheese, along with fresh fruits and vegetables. It was a mix of highly processed foods and the freshest of produce.

My father was an avid gardener and BBQ grill master (aka the Tri-Tip King), so eating cleaner, especially when it came to grilling, was always part of our family life (with the exception of Dad's heavy-handed application of salt and the Crisco and cheese tucked into his famous peppers). Grilling was part of my DNA. We would pick fresh vegetables and fruit from the garden and revolve our meals around what my father had grown the most of . . . normally zucchini. (Thinking back, that's probably why I don't favor it now, as it was a constant on the grill or in sautés when I was growing up.) I always exercised regularly and never struggled with overeating or my weight.

That is, with one exception. For my junior year of high school, I attended the American School in Switzerland. That year abroad was filled with late-night bars and underage drinking, midnight pizzas, fresh-baked Italian rolls with butter and molasses, and daily fresh mozzarella, tomato, and basil sandwiches from the school snack bar. When I returned at the end of the school year ten pounds heavier than my norm, I was not thrilled with myself (though it was worth every minute for the amazing food memories).

My mother, who wanted to help me, took me to the local Diet Center in Santa Barbara, where the plan included overpriced processed foods. My mom had no idea about the dangers of processed foods at the time; she was just doing her best to steer me away from the bread and cheese that led to my weight gain. I spent the summer eating iceberg salads with chemical dressing, and the weight came right off.

It was sort of a blur, and, to be honest, I moved on without much thought. I went off to college with an understanding of how much gluten-laden food I could eat while still maintaining my normal weight. I never really fluctuated by more than five pounds, but I continued to be very swollen in my face, my lower legs, and my stomach. And I had struggled with brain fog my entire life without realizing what it was; I just thought I was sort of a space case. I always felt "off." Those who have experienced it know all too well what I'm talking about: you are off, but no doctor can diagnose the cause. So doctors continued to medicate me with different levels of estrogen birth control pills and other weird shit.

Finally, at eighteen, after requesting more blood tests from the local internist, I was diagnosed with Hashimoto's disease, which is an autoimmune disorder affecting the thyroid gland. Since the thyroid produces hormones to help regulate a lot of your body's functions, feeling sluggish and bloated and off with Hashimoto's is pretty common. This diagnosis was somewhat helpful: I was put on Synthroid to regulate my thyroid, and the symptoms regressed slightly, but there was still the "fog and the puff," so off I went, medicated but still dealing with the fog and "hot face" (again, IYKYK).

In my twenties, I started to do my own research and thought I should cut out gluten to address some of my lingering symptoms. I was working crazy hours as a wardrobe stylist in Los Angeles (insanely early mornings and very late nights on set) and eating tons of fad protein bars, basically repackaged candy bars devoid of any nutritional value. But if they were gluten free, they were fair game. At that point, I was used to feeling puffy and tired.

On a trip to New York, I met a great guy named Kevin, who became the love of my life. I moved to NYC to be with him, and, ready to start feeling better, I researched around for a good endocrinologist, asking everyone I knew in the city for help. I was referred to a doctor who made suggestions that helped change my life, including "Get off the gluten." These were the early days, when gluten intolerance was just starting to be understood. It was Eating for Hashimoto's 101—getting off the gluten was the first step in combating basic inflammation. I felt a lot better, and I am forever grateful for her help.

When I was thirty I was diagnosed with a desmoid tumor (a soft-tissue sarcoma) on my left chest wall and underwent chemotherapy for it. The experience changed me, not only physically but emotionally, too. I learned to care for myself and my body on a different level and appreciated each day a bit more than before. Over the next few years, including during my pregnancies, I focused on eating unprocessed, whole foods daily. No more chemical-filled protein bars.

I had always loved to cook, but now I was doing it more regularly. I realized early on that Kevin had a love for salads, unlike most of the men I know. So dinners would be simple, HUGE salads with vinaigrette, a protein, and a starch, and that was pretty much it, with the exception of tacos . . . another Kevin Fisher favorite. That's why you will see many taco recipes in this book. Kevin also grew up in Southern California, so we share a love for SoCal foods: Simple tacos, big salads, and easy roasted veggies with a protein were always our thing, so when we became parents and I started cooking at home even more, we still kept it simple. Also important to note: Kevin is keto and has been for years, hence his nickname "Keto Kev," and, for those of you who follow my kitchen page, "Coffee Kev" (he delivers me my coffee daily in bed), so he educated me a bit about the "keto life," and I learned to modify recipes and cook specific sides just for him as time went on.

I love cooking for groups, and over the years Thanksgiving has become "my holiday." Years of practicing the Super Bowl of meals, cooking for thirty to forty people, have given me some serious extra kitchen training. I love the holiday so much I have added an extra "Friendsgiving" night into the mix, when I make my turkey tacos and other casual sides (all included in this book). My father has passed, but Thanksgiving will forever be celebrated in his honor at our table, where we share fond memories of him carving the turkey and having one too many vodkas with lemon (also cutting some extremity of his or burning himself). Memories . . . And the apple doesn't fall far from the tree. I'm also known to not be the most graceful member of our family, especially after a cocktail and cooking.

But back to my journey to health. As for a lot of women, after taking excellent care of myself and my eating during my pregnancies, the reality of cooking for kids took over. I always cooked, and as the kids grew, my love of cooking did as well. But the food I cooked for them was always full of dairy and gluten. I wasn't "technically" eating gluten, but would have a bite of the kids' chicken fingers or pizza more often than not, and would open a bottle of wine most nights to drink while I was cooking dinner. Years rolled by, and I was again feeling off constantly. As I aged it started to get worse. I would bloat more easily and wake up most days not feeling mentally clear. If I had had my sugar-filled pinot grigio or rosé the night before, well, forget about it; I would drag through the next day (which was pretty much every day), feeling like shit and exhausted. Only to cycle through it again the next night. Rosé anyone?

Looking back, I see it so clearly now: the repeating cycle of exhaustion, waking multiple times at night (having to pee frequently), intense mood swings, and more. I was zapped of all energy, my pants were always slightly tight, and the bags under my eyes were puffier, as was my moon-shaped face. I just thought this was it and I was aging, so I just had to work out harder and get over it.

But wait, it gets worse. COVID hit. Like many others trapped at home, I really hunkered down, not only for sixty-minute high-intensity Peloton rides but also to cook three huge meals a day, because there was not much else to do, except run my jewelry business remotely. It was then that I discovered a delicious new canned wine from my local artisanal wine store and was cracking one every day at five, when my dinner prep would start. We were all home, so I was making lots of cheesy casseroles and cakes, mainly gluten free but not grain and dairy free, and I wasn't reading labels to check what was in all the products I was using. The bloat, fog, and excessive cardio

(I was legit a hamster on a wheel) continued throughout the pandemic.

My company signed a lease on our first store in Beverly Hills midway through the pandemic and built it out from across the country, sight unseen, to open in February 2021.

Once I was finally cleared to fly to LA, I had to quarantine for ten days (it was high pandemic). I had packed a few books, including one some of my followers had been telling me about by this telehealth doctor in Pennsylvania who specialized in anti-inflammatory living. The book was called *Ketotarian*, and I started it on the plane ride to LA. Mask on and eyes glued and hanging on his every word, I was transformed by the time I landed in California. It was like a lightbulb went off in my head. How had I never thought this way before? It was so simple: Less is more. Read the labels of all you ingest. Remove gluten (OK, easy, I was a pro at that), remove grain (shit, I love rice and quinoa), remove dairy (oh fuck no, not my cheese), remove legumes (OK, those make me fart anyway). Do not ingest seed oils (shit, they are in everything in the US), limit nightshades (OK, don't love eggplant but love jalapeños, so we'll just limit those), and no alcohol (yeah, sorry, not happening, but I'll try organic red wine over the white and rosé), no refined sugar or agave (once I looked, I saw it was even in my favorite hot sauce!). Also no sparkling water (no more "natural flavors," as they are the furthest thing from natural), and one I had not heard of: no gums. Turns out here in the good ole US, gums are in pretty much every prepared food that we eat. Ready to hear what they are? Shelf stabilizers. Yup, preservatives and thickeners to make foods stay fresh longer and not separate. I swell now just thinking of them. When you think about it, it's so nasty. I vowed to give myself three days to try this new way of life, and if it was unbearable I would stop and go back to the roller coaster of my hourlong hamster-wheel workouts, my rosé, and my dairy-filled charcuterie with cane sugar jams.

So there I was in LA at Whole Foods: masked up, stocking up my hotel fridge with any sub I could find that fit into Will Cole's anti-inflammatory equation: I went for the vegan cheese trial first. I think I bought six versions that night, and they all sucked and were inedible, with the exception of two (that are still on my list today). I learned that I could still have "charcuterie"; it just looked slightly different. I scored on some grain-free crackers that were killer. I could still have my cheese, crackers, spreads, and olives and nuts and (organic red) wine; it was just about making different choices, reading the labels on all packaged foods, and being ready to make the commitment to stay in my lane.

Three days went by, and I suddenly woke feeling clearer and lighter (literally). My bloat was disappearing, and I could focus a bit longer. I was hooked. Each day I would hunt like a treasure hunter for new subs at different grocery stores to add into my rotation. I would read labels constantly and started my list of "approved" snacks, canned goods, and packaged foods. It was honestly mind-blowing in the beginning to see how much cane sugar, seed oil, and gums were in almost everything I was consuming.

It was addictive to feel this good, and I wanted to share it with everyone. But I soon found out that not everyone wanted to partake in my new "anti-inflammatory" way of life. My first encounter was in LA when I went to dinner with a group of work friends I hadn't seen since COVID hit. When I ordered my food, I asked for my fish to be cooked in pure olive oil. Everyone at the table stopped talking and looked at me. I had done some online research and discovered that when restaurants say they are using pure olive oil, more often than not it's a blend (of olive and canola, normally), for cost-saving purposes. Some of my friends thought it was amazing I was taking my health into my own hands as I ordered, while others asked for the truffle fries, sort of rolling their eyes and giggling: "OK, Jen . . ."

When the waiter came back to confirm my order, he explained that they did in fact use a blended oil, but the chef could make an exception. A few of my friends jumped in and wanted their food cooked the same way . . . They were also feeling the fatigue and fog and were lost without any real solutions to help. When we spoke further about it that night, most said that their doctors were dismissing their concerns, telling them it's just aging and we have to deal with it. The naysayers at the table said let's see how long this anti-inflammatory way of eating lasts and asked If I could pass the ketchup (enjoy the sugar bloat from that, bitches, lol).

It was that night that gave me the power within myself to stay true to what I felt was right for me. I was just about to turn fifty and realized I wasn't going to roll over and give up. I was going to make it my life to live to the best of my ability and fuck it, let people try to shame me or peer-pressure me for making the choice to care for myself. I am not one to go down without a fight, and this was my new fight. I'd stay true to my choice and continue to educate myself on how to feel better, and if I can look better at the same time, then, boom, that's it for me.

My method for feeling better has changed over time. I've added and modified recipes more and have become more flexible with taking small breaks when I feel I need to eat a piece of pizza or get my favorite Italian spicy pepper Jack cheese or mozzarella sub or the burger with the American cheese and bun. I've found that this flexibility is the key to success. If you want it, eat it. Then go back to the way that makes you feel best.

This entire book is about finding *your* mindset and what works for you. We all crave different things, so it's up to you to modify for yourself. I eat anti-inflammatory food 98 percent of the time now. Days off are normally around my period (obviously), but now that my period journey may be coming to a close soon, I'm just listening to my body more. That's the key to it all: listening to yourself and your body. When you don't listen to this voice, you often find yourself in trouble. You are the decider. The moment you start taking accountability for your actions is when you really get into the zone. Stop blaming your choices on others or on exterior environmental situations. I get messages with excuses from people all the time about why they can't take care of themselves. The most popular are:

"I'm too busy to take the time to shop for all of that."

My answer: "Girl, I'm busy, too. Stop doom-scrolling on your phone and messaging people, and go to the market. You'll get it done in less time than you've used here complaining to me."

"My family won't eat this way, so I can't."

My answer: "Try one of my recipes that incorporate their favorite foods. I always recommend starting with a simple protein or a rice/pasta. Side note: My kids don't eat all these recipes either; that's why they are easy and fast. I make them for myself and let my kids try them."

Excuses are just fear masked by a to-do list, in my opinion, or sometimes simply laziness or a combination of both. If you don't try, you'll never know, and what a shame to live life wondering if things could be different for you. Especially at midlife.

When I turned fifty, I had already begun my midlife "wake-up," or "crisis," or whatever you want to call it—meaning this ride is almost more than half over, and I'd better be grateful for each day. I always try to be productive and move in the direction of doing my best by achieving my dreams and being more honest with myself as well as others. I've really come into myself over the past few years mentally, including learning to voice my direct and honest opinion in all aspects of my life. Yes, maybe my style is too sexy for some, but I'm doing it all while I can and looking my best at the same time. Eating right and caring for my body is huge in this. Maybe I'm too much for some, but that's OK; we probably wouldn't vibe anyway. The same goes for both life and business: I'm less fearful about using my voice and expressing my opinion.

I've also found at this age that being vocal and sharing are helpful for all. Perimenopause is finally being discussed, and if I can help another woman feel better on her journey, then I'm doing something right. My entire goal here is to help women where I didn't have the guidance of a helper. I've found more joy in sharing not only food tips and tricks but also everything I've learned about beauty and clothing, to help others feel better.

Let's talk about something that, thankfully, isn't taboo anymore. Given the fact that my tumor grows from estrogen, I am not necessarily a candidate for HRT. This has made me even more proactive in my efforts to find new ways to cope with my changing body and mind without hormone therapy. I've been trying new vitamins and peptides, but I'm early in, and we can talk about this more once I'm in menopause—I know I will remain curious and vocal until my last breath.

ON EATING OUT

Restaurant meals and takeout can be a challenge when you're following an anti-inflammatory way of eating. Restaurants often use sneaky oils and other inflammatory ingredients. The first thing I recommend is to stop ordering takeout unless you know it's from a reputable, seed oil–free restaurant (my favorite in NYC is Locanut). But if takeout is the only option, I try to stick to build-your-own salads with fresh-squeezed lemon or lime and pure olive oil as your dressing. Proteins that are added on can be sneaky, too, because you can't guarantee what they have been cooked in. If I'm not sure, I'll still add an egg or egg whites, and shrimp if it looks poached, and load up on low-sugar vegetables. My favorites are fresh jalapeños, cucumbers, red onion, and cilantro, to complement whatever protein I can get my hands on. If the protein is not looking great, I add beans—not my go-to, because of the whole bloating issue, but still better than feeling skeeved out by the meat.

When I go out to lunch or dinner with friends or for work, I like Mediterranean restaurants where I can get a piece of wood-fired fish cooked only in olive oil, sushi restaurants where I can get sashimi, a good bistro where I can get a really good (grass-fed!) burger without a bun or roasted chicken (make sure they don't use vegetable or canola oil on the grill!), or a brasserie with a raw bar. I love loading up on oysters and shrimp cocktail (sans the sugary cocktail sauce). My most important advice for eating out is to be kind to whoever is helping you at the table and explain how you eat clearly, as they will be more sympathetic to ask for your subs when needed. If they understand how cooking the food in certain oils makes you feel, they tend to be incredibly helpful.

A LITTLE MORE PROTEIN

Protein is having a real Moment right now. Here is how I get it: I eat a lot of seafood, chicken, and turkey rather than red meat. I love red meat but don't love how it makes me feel the next day. One of my favorite meals used to be a nice juicy steak, but my body doesn't metabolize it as well as it used to. I eat a lot of eggs, sometimes with yolks, sometimes *not*. Tinned fish and a ton of my meatballs. Nuts. If you are having a salad, add kale. I am not a smoothie gal. I know that smoothies are a great source of protein, and if you can find the right protein powder for you, Godspeed. I just truly prefer to chew my food. I'm not satisfied if I drink a meal.

SPICES

READY, SET, GO! SHOPPING AND STOCKING YOUR PANTRY

YOUR FREEZER IS YOUR FRIEND

I encourage you to make use of your freezer! I keep most of my proteins in there so I always have what I need on hand. If I want salmon in the a.m., I pull a piece out and defrost it. Same goes for ground meat, chicken, grain-free bread, and bagels for the kids. I don't have a huge freezer in NYC, so I keep it tight.

Here's a list of essentials I keep stocked in the freezer to help sustain my wholesome anti-inflammatory diet with ease.

FREEZER MUST-HAVES:

Wild-caught shrimp

Wild-caught scallops

Wild-caught salmon
(individually packed servings; I like FreshDirect or Whole Foods sockeye)

Wild-caught tilapia—
my fave for fish tacos! (individually packed servings; I like FreshDirect)

Wild-caught cod

2 packs (11/4 pounds/544 g each) organic chicken wings

Organic chicken thighs

Organic chicken breasts

2 packs (1 pound/455 g each) skirt steak

1 pound (455 g) organic ground beef

2 pounds (910 g) organic ground chicken and turkey

Bacon
(If I'm not making the entire thing, I cut the bacon slices in half and freeze about eight half-slices in individual bags to pull out for breakfasts or other recipes)

Organic riced cauliflower
(I like the 365 brand in 24-ounce/910 g bags)

Organic butternut squash

Organic chopped spinach

Organic chopped kale

Trader Joe's charred corn

Trader Joe's artichoke hearts

Organic petite peas

Organic chopped kale

AWG Loaves—
my favorite flavors are everything and rosemary (I slice the loaves, then freeze them so I can pull out slices as needed)

AWG Rounds
(my favorite for mini pizzas)

AWG Everything Bagels

Regular bagels—for the kids
(I get them at Utopia Bagels)

Cassava tortillas (I love Coyotas)

Trader Joe's cauliflower gnocchi

Trader Joe's turkey burgers

Ice cream—vanilla, chocolate chip, cookies and cream

Vodka

TOOLS FOR SUCCESS

I'm a big believer in not buying extra cooking gadgets you don't need and won't use. You will not see an avocado slicer or a garlic peeler listed here. Don't buy the new gadget that's trending on social media just because everyone else is, if you don't actually need it to make your regular recipe rotation. Save your money and buy an extra pair of shoes instead. But cooking in a kitchen without the proper basics is like going to school without a backpack, so invest in the essential appliances and tools, then build on those essentials based on what you love to cook or bake. On to the basics . . .

I cannot say this loud enough: You are nothing without SHARP KNIVES in your kitchen. Don't f@!% around with cheap, dull knives. Waste of time. Quality sharp knives are the number-one most important tool for your kitchen. And you don't have to spend a fortune—just don't buy the ones hanging in houseware stores in the impossible-to-open plastic hanging thing. Material Kitchen (no, I'm not paid by them, but I should be) makes awesome affordable knives. Get the 8-inch (20 cm) chef's knife, the 6-inch (15 cm) serrated knife, and the paring knife. I also love a 6-inch (15 cm) utility knife and a flat chopper.

"Main drawer" basics and must-haves, IMO, include a mandoline, a can opener, a vegetable peeler, measuring spoons, measuring cups (dry), a citrus reamer, a lemon/lime squeezer, a small mesh strainer, whisks (metal and rubber), silicone spatulas (not black), a fish spatula, a metal flattop spatula, a silicone brush, a microplane zester, tongs (long and short), a digital food thermometer, a cheese grater (fine and coarse), a poultry pounder, a slotted spoon, wooden spoons in varied styles, a ladle, kitchen shears, toothpicks, a pepper grinder, a mortar and pestle, and a rolling pin.

"Extra gadgets" that you don't really need and use maybe once a year, but when you need them it's nice to have them: an ice cream scoop, a cherry pitter, seafood forks, caviar spoons, lobster crackers, a pizza cutter, a gas brûlée flame, biscuit cutters, a veggie spiralizer, a cookie scoop, a cookie press, a garlic press, a latte blender, a zigzag food chopper (great if you have kids—it gets them to eat their raw veggies), and cookie cutters. (When my kids were younger, I had a ton of them; now I have a heart and a star . . . honestly, all you ever need; they just want to frost everything at a certain age, so save your money on the unicorn- and truck-shaped cutters. They really don't care.)

Bigger things that are essential, like a salad spinner, a colander, a large-mesh sieve, baking sheets (various sizes), wire racks (baking/nonstick and cooking), a large sheet tray, a nonstick loaf pan, a bundt pan, a pie dish, a muffin tray (I have two), a wooden cutting board, a regular frying pan, and a smaller nonstick frying pan.

The "biggies" (aka appliances and plugins): Only buy what you know you will use, as this shiz takes up a ton of space (especially if you live in an apartment in NYC). The biggies include a stand mixer, a hand mixer, an immersion blender, a blender, a food processor, a slow cooker, an Instant Pot, an air fryer (I threw mine out, as convection baking is sort of the same to me and all the air fryers have too small an interior, IMO), a coffee and/or spice grinder, a toaster and/or toaster oven, a waffle maker, and a coffeemaker (not mentioning the obvious, like a microwave and an oven).

Disposables: unbleached parchment paper, baking cups, and cotton twine; cheesecloth, foil, and plastic wrap.

Yes, I know I have probably missed things (thank god you can't DM me telling me right now . . . but I'm sure you will later).

JENNIFER FISHER SALTS

I highly recommend all of my salts. No surprise there.

For those who don't know the backstory of Jennifer Fisher Salts—"I thought she was a jewelry designer . . . why is she making salt? This is weird"—you are right, it is sort of weird . . . but so am I. So why not? It's just who I am . . . People scratch their heads and ask why a jewelry designer would make salt, not shoes or handbags first. It's not unlike how my jewelry brand started: I couldn't find what I was looking for, so I made my own.

I created my first seasoned salt, "Universal Salt," because I didn't want any garlic or onion in my food when I was cooking myself breakfast in the morning. I searched high and low, all over the land (meaning every specialty grocery store in NYC and LA), with no luck. So when I couldn't find what I was craving and saw what was missing in the market, I decided to make my own. My Universal Salt consists of kosher salt, black pepper, dill weed, dried cilantro, red pepper flakes, and lemon zest. Why lemon zest? Growing up near Santa Barbara, California (Montecito to be exact), I had no shortage of lemons or avocados (which is why I use them so much in my recipes). After I moved from Los Angeles to NYC, my father used to pick lemons from his trees (or from other trees around town) and ship me boxes of them, so I would always have fresh lemons in my house. Never wanting to waste any part of them, I would zest their exteriors and dry the lemon flesh to be used in recipes.

I couldn't find the perfect seasoning for my breakfast: most were BBQ rubs or too fancy-smelling, like potpourri . . . nothing I wanted my eggs to taste like. So I made a small bowl of all my favorite seasonings and flavors that I did want my eggs to taste like, and the result was, inevitably, JF Universal Salt. I was an early adopter of Instagram, and one day I didn't have any content to post, so I posted my poached egg avocado toast, as one did back in the day. Little did I know how people would respond. This was before DMs, so suddenly my comments were flooded with (A) "Wait, you can cook and poach an egg?" and (B) "What is that seasoning?" It literally got more comments and likes than the major celebrity wearing my jewelry in the previous post. Food instantly resonated with my followers . . . If you think about it, we put our jewelry on once a day, but we eat three times a day (if you don't intermittently fast), so it made perfect sense. Others were looking for the perfect seasoned salt too, and, like me, people enjoy simple food. That's when I began to share more of my cooking publicly and started my food-based Instagram—@Maedyn—because I wanted to keep my food and my jewelry separate.

Soon after the Universal salt came Spicy Salt, my favorite, and then Curry Salt (the sleeper favorite to serve over avocados, tomatoes or eggs). The newest addition, Everything Style Spicy Salt, is my favorite for seasoning roasted vegetables and chicken wings.

Thank You for Shopping With Us

THE JF GROCERY LIST

OK . . . grocery shopping. As a working mom in NYC, I take full advantage of FreshDirect Express to deliver what I need to make dinner. I also live next to a Whole Foods and regularly walk past many corner stores that stock fresh organic produce. Now that my kids are older, I've stopped shopping daily for huge dinners. I do, however, shop every two or three days for fresh vegetables that have a short shelf life.

I'm well aware how very lucky I am to live in a city with so many resources. Many people don't have such easy access to fresh organic produce and ingredients. That's not lost on me. When these options aren't available, it's just a matter of making the most of the ingredients you have on hand and can access. The "nonnegotiables" I always have on hand are listed below. Consider this list a basic cheat sheet of bare-bones fresh-fridge essentials. These are things I can make a meal out of at any time of day, whatever my mood, so there are never any instances when I'm not able to figure something out (using my already stocked pantry and freezer staples), even if I'm feeling lazy or tired. Keep in mind that this list contains "fresh" ingredients only; I am not including items already in my fridge with a longer shelf life, or in my pantry or freezer.

MY BASIC TWO- TO THREE-DAY SHOP

2 proteins—normally a ground meat (typically chicken and turkey) and a cut of red meat, chicken, or pork

Soy-free organic eggs (that means eggs from hens who are fed a diet free of soy or corn)

Avocados

Organic romaine lettuce

Garlic (not that garbage in a jar, the real cloves)

White onion/red onion/green onion

Organic Persian cucumbers

Organic lemons

Organic limes

Bananas

Organic strawberries

Organic blueberries

Organic raspberries

Every week I replenish my organic cilantro, flat-leaf parsley, and dill. I'll alternate a few veggies here and there depending on seasonality and my mood, but if I have the things on this list replenished every two or three days and I do one larger shop for vegetables with a longer shelf life (sweet potatoes, cabbage, celery, tomatoes, and fruits), I'm good.

SPICES

The spice cabinet. Your arsenal of shelf-stable flavors. Your key to adding flavor without using fresh herbs. The list will vary based on your personal favorites. This is my list . . . it may not be your list. I'll say this a lot in this book. What I love, you might not love, so change it. It's your kitchen. Cooking is all about figuring out YOUR favorite flavor profiles, not mimicking what others tell you is right or essential. I made that mistake early on, purchasing useless random spices that were deemed "essential," only to end up shoving them to the back of my cabinet, unused and eventually thrown out.

Here's my list of basic dried herbs and essential seasonings:

I mean obviously JF Salt . . . all flavors

Freshly cracked black pepper (not the precracked flavorless dust I'll sometimes find when I'm trying to cook at a friend's house or in an office)

Garlic powder

Onion powder

Dried parsley

Dried basil

Dried dill

Ground cumin

Paprika, smoked and sweet (regular)

Dried thyme

Dried cilantro

Crushed red pepper

Dried oregano

Ground coriander

Dried rosemary

Dried mint

Dried sage

Dried tarragon

Dried celery seed

Caraway seeds

Curry powder

Saffron

Bay leaves

Turmeric

Poppy seeds

Sesame seeds (black and white)

Minced garlic

Minced onion

Cardamom pods

Cayenne pepper

Wild za'atar

Chinese five-spice powder

Dried ground ginger

Ground cinnamon

Ground nutmeg

Ground cloves

Whole cloves

Cream of tartar

Ground allspice

Anise

Mustard seed

Aleppo pepper

Cobanero chili flakes

Coarse salt

Kosher salt

Dried mustard powder

Old Bay Seasoning

THE ART OF SNACKING

So this has little to do with cooking, but I feel it's an important bonus to include, because part of the success of eating and feeling better is snacking better. I would feel remiss if I didn't give you guys this juicy tidbit as part of my work here. I love to snack, and I was doing it all wrong before I started on my path of anti-inflammatory eating. Before I learned how to snack right, I was a Babybel cheese wheel addict who was also eating safflower- and palm oil-filled chips and seaweed. My snack list has evolved over the years, especially when new products came on the market, but the following are constants that have been in the mix for travel and work for a while. Bravo to all the companies that actually care what we ingest and are constantly innovating this part of the food market for us. Note that the specific brands and flavors I share below are important (as with all other packaged foods), because brands can be sneaky and serve you seed oils and cane sugar in the fine print in many alternative flavors.

PROTEIN-PACKED SNACKS

The New Primal Meat Sticks: My favorites are Chicken & Maple, Buffalo Chicken, and Vermont Smoke & Cure Uncured Turkey Pepperoni Sticks. I use these easy-to-pack snacks to up my protein. They're great for plane travel, because they deliver protein without liquids (or the smell of eggs or tuna). And one of these sticks (the kid-size version) is a perfect portion, because you can enjoy a meat stick and another small snack at the same time.

B.T.R. Nation Protein Bars: My fave is Dark Chocolate Brownie Recharge.

Baked Pork Rinds: I love the Epic Provisions Pink Himalayan Sea Salt flavor.

DRIED FRUITS AND NUTS

RIND Snacks Skin-On Dried Fruit: This company makes amazing mixes of simply dried fruits in interesting varieties, as well as simply dried coconut. I always bring a bag of one of them when I travel.

Frühling Nocciola: Their hazelnut and chocolate combo is my favorite nut mix. It is hands-down the best combination of dried fruit and nuts on the market. It's not largely available commercially and is artisanal in its mix of ingredients. They also make a superior dried mango.

Rancho Meladuco Organic Medjool Dates: IYKYK, these are superior in farming and manufacturing. They come from Palm Springs in boxes and are the perfect snack for flights. I add them to my own raw nut mixes (I love hazelnuts, almonds, and Brazil nuts) along with coconut-sugar chocolate chips.

Daily Crunch Sprouted Nuts: These are amazing once you get used to the texture of sprouted nuts. If you are reading this and you follow how I eat, I'm sure you will love these too. My favorite flavors are the Cacao + Sea Salt, the Dill Pickle (sleeper . . . amazing), and the Nashville Hot.

OTHER MUNCHABLES

Elemental Superfoods Bars: My favorite flavors of these are the Double Chocolate + Reishi, Chaga & Cordyceps, and Mulberry, Cacao + Spirulina Bars.

Gimme Seaweed (Avocado Oil and Olive Oil): My fave is the avocado oil version. I use these as wraps for most of my lunches; they also make a "big sheet" version.

Grain-Free Granola: I like Hampton Grocer Superseed Granola and Purely Elizabeth Grain-Free Granola.

Simple Mills crackers: I go for their everything seed crackers, black pepper crackers, and rosemary crackers, and if I'm dying for a Cheez-It vibe I'll do the cheddar crackers.

Simple Mills cookies: I love the graham and chocolate graham cookies. These are my kryptonite; I can't keep them stocked in the house. (Good luck not eating the whole box in front of the TV!)

Siete Grain Free Tortilla Chips (available in serving-size bags).

Boulder Canyon Avocado Oil Kettle-Cooked Potato Chips (available in serving-size bags).

Green olives: Divina Market sells them in serving-size packs.

These are the snack basics that are always with me on long car rides and for plane travel as well as at my office. Work is a sneaky place where stress and lack of time can drive you to make not the best choices (cue an office birthday cake and a.m. doughnuts). I make sure I allow space for snacks during meetings and throughout the day, in case lunch isn't happening due to meetings or other time constraints.

PANTRY STAPLES

A well-stocked pantry will be your best friend. Pantries are not just for snacks and emergency cans of tomatoes. I use my pantry as a "garage" (maybe not the most inviting term, but it's true) for all the items I could possibly want or need to make anything at a moment's notice.

I organize my pantry meticulously. I know this is a trend—you can find endless suggestions and products to help you arrange your own pantry to your liking. The key to me is the contents of my pantry, which I've separated into lists by category for you below. My main goal is to stock my kitchen with things that are gum-, sugar-, and seed oil–free. My subs may not be perfect for everyone, but as I always say, this is what works for me. There are products that might not work for you, and that's OK—find your version.

Please note: There will be some dupes in my pantry list and fridge list, cases where I keep one in the fridge at all times and an extra in the pantry. Also, this pantry list does not include my snacks. For my snacking recommendations, see page 32.

PANTRY "LIQUIDS" OR THINGS PACKED IN LIQUID

Kettle & Fire Low Sodium Vegetable, Chicken, and Beef Broth

Imagine Chicken Broth: I buy this in four-packs of 1 cup/240 ml serving each

Native Forest, Trader Joe's, or Let's Do Organic Coconut Cream and Coconut Milk: Always read the labels, as some versions, especially Native Forest, may contain hidden gums.

Muir Glen or any organic diced tomatoes

Whole canned tomatoes

SAUCES AND PASTES

Thai Kitchen red curry paste

Mekhala yellow curry paste

Mike's Organic Curry Love green curry paste

Muir Glen or any organic tomato sauce (I like the 8-ounce/225 g cans)

NON-GRAIN NOODLES

Sea Tangle Kelp Noodles

Jovial Grain Free cassava pasta: penne, orzo, fusilli, and spaghetti

Natural Heaven Hearts of Palm Lasagne and Linguini

TINNED FISH / PROTEIN

Wild Planet low-sodium albacore and skipjack tuna

Tonnino tuna in olive oil (I also love the glass jars of the flavored versions: jalapeño and oregano are my faves)

Mina sardines (great protein in a pinch on crackers with lots of fresh lemon and slices of fresh jalapeño)

Wild Planet organic roasted chicken (makes for a great protein crust or bread)

CANNED VEGGIES

Native Forest hearts of palm in water

Native Forest artichoke hearts in water

Native Forest water chestnuts

Mementa Organic Young Jackfruit (a great sub for seitan or tofu)

365 Black Olives (can't help it, it's a childhood favorite: the bland black olive)

Divina Frescatrano Olives

Divina Castelvetrano Olives

Divina Kalamata Olives (I also like Kosterina brand kalamatas)

Jeff's Garden Pickled Jalapeño Peppers

Jeff's Garden Hot Cherry Peppers

Jeff's Garden Golden Greek Pepperoncini

Diced green chiles

Pimentos

NUTS, SEEDS, AND DRIED FRUIT

Organic raw cashews

Organic raw almonds

Slivered almonds

Raw sunflower seeds

Dried organic figs

Dried organic apricots

Organic raw pumpkin seeds

Organic raw macadamia nuts

Organic flaxseeds

FLOURS AND SUGARS

Almond flour (I like Bob's Red Mill)

Cassava flour (I like Bob's Red Mill)

Arrowroot flour (I like Bob's Red Mill)

Coconut sugar (I like Big Tree Farms vanilla coconut sugar)

Brown coconut sugar (I like Big Tree Farms)

OILS, VINEGARS, AND SAUCES

The slippery suckers . . . oils and vinegars, aka pantry lubrication. I love a variety of oils but use olive and avocado oils the most. For vinegar, I'm a red wine gal most of the time.

Olive oil (favorites are Kyoord, Kosterina, and Fancy Peasant)

Avocado oil

Coconut oil (refined and unrefined)

Sesame oil

Toasted sesame oil

Zero Acre Cultured Cooking Oil (close to vegetable oil but clean)

Red wine vinegar

White wine vinegar

Champagne vinegar

Balsamic vinegar

Apple cider vinegar

White vinegar (the stuff you clean with)

Sherry vinegar

Rice wine vinegar

Fig balsamic glaze

"REFRIGERATE AFTER OPENING" CONDIMENTS

My favorite food "lubricants" are condiments—hot sauce and mustard being at the top of my list. I have a thing for them. They add a fast and easy depth of flavor to everything and are just as important to meals as other ingredients, in my non-chef, untrained personal opinion.

Tia Lupita Hot Sauce (The O.G. Red version): A healthier version of Taco Bell medium hot sauce. I grew up on the Bell, and the hot-sauce flavor profile will forever be a favorite. Get this sauce—it's amazing. I love it drizzled over my spa tuna (page 92) or scooped up on a tortilla chip.

Siete Botana Jalapeño Sauce

Frank's Red Hot Original Cayenne Pepper Sauce

Tabasco Sauce

Yellowbird Sriracha

Primal Kitchen Original Buffalo Sauce

Coconut Secret Coconut Aminos Garlic and Teriyaki Sauce (soy-free, with minimal ingredients)

Primal Kitchen Ketchup

Noble Made Less-Sugar and Smoky BBQ Sauce

Primal Kitchen Spicy Brown Mustard

Organicville Dijon Mustard

Primal Kitchen No Dairy Queso

Everiday Chili Crisp

Everiday House Red Chili Hot Sauce

Plus a couple of fridge staples: Organic concentrated tomato paste and chili paste

BAKING INGREDIENTS

I'm a very simple baker, but when I have the time I love to bake. Here are the basics to have on hand to make all the baked goods in this book.

Baking soda

Baking powder

All-purpose flour

Blanched almond flour

Honey

Maple syrup

Vanilla coconut sugar

Coconut sugar

Brown coconut sugar

Powdered sugar

Organic cane sugar

Brown sugar

Maple or date sugar (optional)

Organic tapioca flour

Organic coconut flour

Corn flour

Arrowroot flour

Vanilla extract (I like Beyond Good . . . your fave might contain cane sugar or be filled with garbage, so read the labels)

Organic cocoa powder

Chocolate chips, regular and mini (I like Hu Kitchen; Guittard also makes a coconut sugar–sweetened version)

Unsweetened chocolate

LUNCH TO GO

TRAVEL OR WORKING LUNCHES

I have a hard rule when I travel. I don't eat plane food unless there is an emergency; e.g., I didn't have time to prep ahead, or I really want to try the international menu. Yes, many airlines have improved their menus, but I still like to pack my own food when I'm traveling. My current favorite is the Bonberi x Jennifer Fisher NYFW survival salad, or any salad I can pack in a disposable, compostable container.

JAR SALADS

I started making jar salads because I was underwhelmed with the serving size of protein from traditional takeout salad restaurants. I would find myself picking the protein out, to be left with a big bowl of underdressed greens. Not to mention the cost. I wanted to include an entire section on this, because they are so popular, but in reality any salad can be a "jar salad"—it is all in how you pack it. The keys to an easily transportable working-lunch salad are the layering and the assembly. The first rule of a jar salad is dressing on the bottom. Then you build your salad, starting with the heartiest ingredients on the bottom that won't absorb the dressing. Avocado and cabbage are my favorite base layers, followed by protein and cheese, then topped with the more delicate greens and finished with herbs so they don't wilt. This results in a "sog and spill-free" fresh salad every time. There's nothing worse than spilled dressing in a designer handbag. Trust me, I've been there. RIP that one Celine tote. I couldn't unsee that small oil ring and had to sell it. Note to self: Pack your own salad in a 24-ounce (720 ml) leak-free glass container from Amazon, and be sure to close it securely.

I feel better when I pack my own lunch. It's always better than any salad you order that skimps on the avocado or dressing. Packing your lunch is cool. Learn to do it. Also, don't be afraid of including leftovers. Cut-up chicken meatballs are insanely delish in a salad the next day, not to mention cut-up Mom's Not Lazy, Lazy Chicken (page 167), and pretty much every recipe in this book. We have to survive and nourish ourselves, so why not take five and pack a perfect lunch for yourself? You can even do it the night before in most cases, so you just have to grab it and go in the a.m. (Pro tip: Leave a note for yourself by the front door so you don't forget it; nothing worse than that feeling.)

KEEPING IT SIMPLE WHEN IT COMES TO SUPPLEMENTS

I would be remiss to not mention the following supplements, as they are part of my life. I am no doctor or wellness practitioner—you should talk to your doctor before starting any supplement regimen—but since I get asked about my own supplements, I will list what I take.

Every day I start with . . .

Prana by Leefy Organics Turmeric, Ginger, and Black Pepper Tincture (for inflammation support)

Sarah Wragge Wellness Alkalize—Detoxifying Greens Powder

Shore Magic: marine collagen (I add this to my coffee)

Then my handful of vitamins:

Kinder Thoughts Saffron Supplement by The Fullest (it helps my mood)

Time Line Mitopure Longevity Supplement (for cell renewal and antiaging)

Lumity Female Dietary Supplement, a.m. and p.m. versions (my multi-vitamin)

Nue Co Skin Filter Supplement

Nue Co Growth Phase Supplement (for hair)

Nue Co Mushroom Mu Complex (for focus)

Fatty15 Supplement (essential fatty acids)

BodyBio, PC, Liposomal Phospholipid Complex

Body Bio Gut+ Prebiotic and Postbiotic

Femmenessence PRO PERI Symphony Natural Health (hormone balance for perimenopause)

Thorne or Arrae Creatine

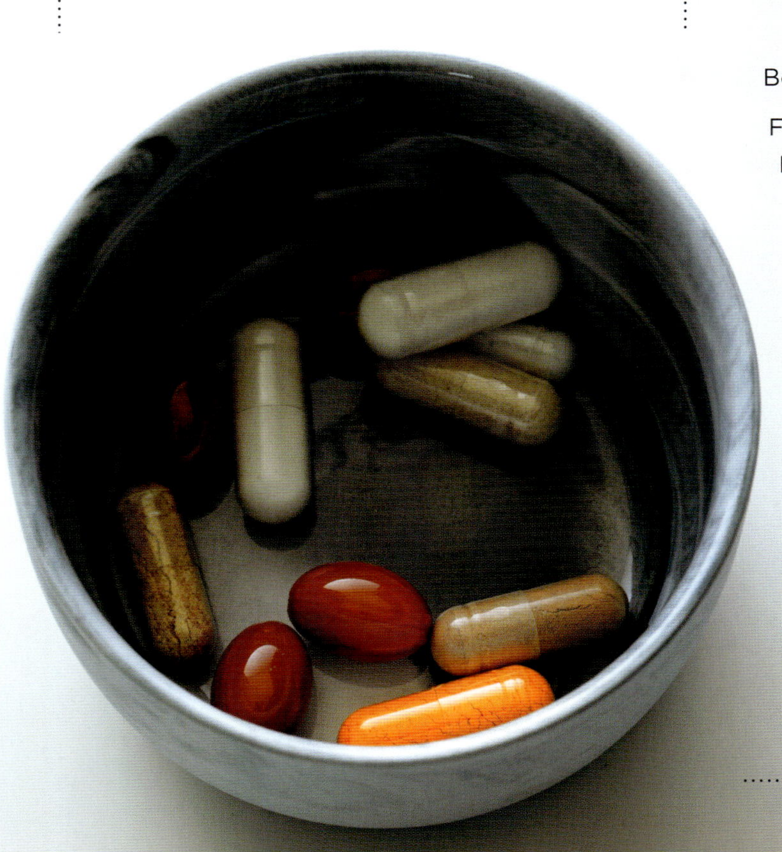

DON'T BE FOOLED BY COFFEE OR SPECIALTY COFFEE DRINKS

It's sort of insane how hard it is to get a creamy cup of coffee anywhere that isn't laden with gums, refined sugar, or dairy. Do what I do and buy compostable coffee cups from Amazon and make your own coffee to go.

I don't love super-sweet coffee, so I sweeten my coffee with vanilla coconut sugar and top with warmed almond milk with a pinch of cinnamon. It's become a ritual for me to pack my own joe to go. I wait to get to my office to make my second cup (or sub a Warm Feelings Saffron Latte from the Fullest).

Before traveling, I prepack tiny bags of my Big Sky Farms vanilla coconut sugar, two scoops of Shore Magic marine collagen powder, and a pinch of Burlap & Barrel cinnamon. In fact, this is such a routine that I've posted about it, and people are constantly asking me to package this concoction the way I have my salts.

Never say never, but for now you can pack your own the way I've described above. If I'm in a pinch, I drink black coffee.

BOOZE

I know this is a loaded thing for many in many different ways, so I'll just say one thing: I choose to drink alcohol. Do I feel better when I don't? A resounding YES. Does it affect me more than it used to? Yes, but that also depends on how much I consume. Some nights, especially at work events, I don't drink. (More on that later, along with my recipe for my special "fake drink" for parties if you don't feel like drinking.)

As mentioned earlier, I used to be a huge rosé and pinot grigio consumer or, when out, a vodka martini gal (no vermouth), and I lived for a freshly stuffed blue cheese olive. It was my thing for years. But I found as time went on that I wasn't very nice or very clear when I drank vodka, so I reluctantly switched to tequila. The result when I changed was sort of mind-blowing. I was nicer to all while drinking and I didn't feel the same instant blur, angst, or "hangxiety."

Now my current drink of choice is an additive-free tequila. (If you check online, you might be surprised to see that your favorite blanco has additives.) I like mine shaken with lots of fresh lime (like a whole lime's worth) and jalapeño, if available, with a spicy rim. I steer clear of the spicy elixirs many specialty cocktail bars offer just because I prefer a fresh chile pepper or jalapeño. Every so often I'll opt for a straight vodka martini (I'm not a vermouth fan), and if I'm at Mr. Chow, I'll get a touch of lychee juice on the side so I can literally add a splash for flavor.

Sometimes I'll get a hankering for a Negroni, especially if I'm in Europe and they can't nail the spicy margarita. No, I don't count the sugar in my alcohol. A drink is a drink to me and actually like a dessert in most cases. When the dessert menu comes, I opt just to finish my drink.

I talk about the importance of organic red wine when I started my journey (see page 15), and I do love the taste of red wine. But I now steer clear of any white wine or rosé and often champagne, because honestly I don't love the taste anymore. I sort of got PTSD from all my white wine–filled days into nights during COVID.

Jammy Eggs

I eat prob eight of these a week. This recipe is so quick and easy and always yields the perfect jammy egg. Great for office lunches or used as a salad topper, and a delicious bite seasoned with kosher salt (or sub JF Spicy Salt)! Pro tip: I add a little oil to the boiling water, as it really helps with the peeling post-boiling. Also fun fact: Eggs are porous, so the oil creates a layer between the egg shell and membrane, making peeling eggs a dream. **MAKES 12 EGG HALVES**

INGREDIENTS

6 large eggs, cold

1 teaspoon olive oil or avocado oil

PROCESS

1 Fill a large bowl with cold water and some ice. Set aside. In a saucepan large enough to fit 6 eggs, bring 4 to 5 inches (10 to 12 cm) of water plus the oil to a boil. Gently submerge your eggs into the boiling water using a slotted spoon and cover the pot. Boil for 6 minutes, then use the slotted spoon to remove the eggs to the ice bath to stop the cooking process.

2 To eat, lightly tap the shell of an egg against a flat surface and carefully lift the shell off the whites. Any leftover eggs will keep refrigerated, in their shells in an airtight container, for about 3 days.

Grain-Free Vanilla Cinnamon Granola

Yes, oats are gluten free, but I made a decision to cut them from my plan early on, along with all of the other grains I was ingesting. But I was bummed when I cut the oats from my life, and I had a hard time finding the perfect replacement for my favorite oat-filled granola. So out of frustration, I started messing around to make my own. This is the result.

This new favorite is slightly chunkier than the norm intentionally, making it ideal to snack on or add to a breakfast bowl with yogurt and fresh fruit. I pack this for airplane trips and or long car rides. Better than the packaged stuff, and you can customize to suit your own taste.

If you are still buying grain-free granola, make sure to read the labels carefully. Many times there is added agave or other sugars, along with other grains like puffed rice and quinoa. That is another reason I just prefer to make this granola at home, so I always have some on hand.

Feel free to truly make this your own by adding dried fruits or nuts of your choice. **SERVES 4**

INGREDIENTS

- 2 tablespoons almond butter
- 1 teaspoon kosher salt, or sub JF Spicy Salt
- ¼ cup (60 ml) maple syrup
- 2 tablespoons ground cinnamon
- 1 teaspoon pure vanilla extract
- 2 cups (220 g) slivered almonds (use sliced almonds if you want a more delicately textured granola)
- 1 cup (85 g) unsweetened shredded coconut
- 2 tablespoons ground flaxseeds (flaxseed meal)
- ½ cup (60 g) dried blueberries or dried fruit or nuts of choice (optional)

PROCESS

1 Preheat the oven to 325°F (165°C). Line a small baking sheet with aluminum foil.

2 In a large bowl, gently mix the almond butter, salt, maple syrup, cinnamon, and vanilla, using a rubber spatula to slightly loosen up the almond butter. Add the almonds, coconut, and ground flaxseeds. Mix well with your hands. The mixture will have large clumps that will crisp in the oven—you can break those up once the granola is baked.

3 Spread the mixture in an even layer on the prepared baking sheet and bake until crisp and golden, 20 to 25 minutes. You can go longer if you'd like your granola to be more browned, but be sure to keep a close eye so it doesn't overbake.

4 Once baked, remove from the oven and let sit on the pan until cool enough to handle. Break the granola up into bite-size pieces. Store in an airtight container for up to 1 week.

Marinated Eggs

These marinated eggs are super easy and versatile. You start with the Jammy Eggs recipe (page 49) and soak them in a coconut amino and garlic-jalapeño marinade overnight. They're excellent served over cauliflower rice alongside tangy-spicy kimchi. You can also add them as a perfect protein to my late-night kelp noodles (page 197) or "takeout" cauliflower rice (page 131). The coconut aminos and garlic give these eggs the best flavor; they're delish cold with a pinch of extra salt on each side of the yolk. **MAKES 12 EGG HALVES**

INGREDIENTS

6 Jammy Eggs (page 49), peeled

½ cup (120 ml) coconut aminos

½ teaspoon kosher salt, or sub JF Spicy Salt

1 teaspoon black and white sesame seeds

1 clove garlic, minced

2 green onions, sliced

¼ jalapeño chile, seeded and chopped

PROCESS

In a large container with an airtight lid, combine ½ cup (120 ml) water, the coconut aminos, salt, sesame seeds, garlic, green onions, and jalapeño. Nestle the eggs in the marinade. Cover with the lid and refrigerate overnight. The next day, discard the marinade. Slice the eggs in half when you're ready to eat them.

LAGUIOLE
FRANCE

Santa Barbara-Style Eggs

This recipe is an homage to my hometown and my father's garden in Santa Barbara, and a testament to my love for Mexican food. I have fond memories of the tomatoes and peppers always growing in my dad's garden. There's a ton of both of those things in this recipe, which serves as a great alternative to a heavy breakfast burrito—you can think of it as a deconstructed one! It also makes an amazing hangover breakfast. Use fried eggs as shown here or scramble a few and add in the veggies for a fast deconstructed omelette. **SERVES 2 TO 4**

INGREDIENTS

1 tablespoon olive oil

¼ cup (30 g) chopped red onion

1 green onion, thinly sliced

1 medium tomato, seeded and chopped

1 jalapeño chile, seeded and chopped

6 to 8 large eggs

Kosher salt, or JF Spicy Salt

6 to 8 tortillas (I like Coyotas)

½ avocado, pitted, peeled, and sliced

1 tablespoon dairy-free sour cream or plain coconut yogurt

Handful chopped fresh cilantro

1 lime, cut into wedges

Freshly cracked black pepper

Hot sauce, for serving

PROCESS

1 Heat the olive oil in a large skillet over medium heat. Add the red onions, green onions, tomatoes, and jalapeño and sauté for 2 to 3 minutes, until softened.

2 In a large bowl, whisk the eggs together, then add to the pan. Reduce the heat to low and cook until the edges are just barely set but the center of the eggs are still raw. Using a rubber spatula, gently swipe across and around the pan to create large soft curds. Continue repeating this motion, pausing for a few seconds in between to allow the curds to set—the entire process should take just 3 to 4 minutes. Season with salt. Remove from the heat and set the pan aside while you char the tortillas.

3 I like to char my tortillas over an open gas flame for extra flavor. Using metal tongs over a medium flame, char both sides evenly, flipping a few times. Careful not to burn them!

4 Divide the scrambled eggs among the charred corn tortillas. Top each one with some avocado slices and a spoonful of sour cream. Garnish with the cilantro and a lime wedge. Season with salt, freshly cracked black pepper, and your favorite hot sauce.

My Kind of Bars

I had a difficult time finding the exact flavors I wanted in a sweet snack that was portable, so I created my own clean version of a granola bar. Think of them as the anti-garbage grab-and-go protein bar. You can pronounce everything in these, and they are also freakin' delish. Use this recipe as the base to create your own favorite version. Some people like more or zero coconut; some will want extra chocolate chips or cinnamon. You do you here. **MAKES ABOUT 24 BARS**

INGREDIENTS

½ cup (65 g) raw pumpkin seeds

½ cup (70 g) raw sunflower seeds

½ cup (50 g) sliced almonds

½ cup (45 g) unsweetened shredded coconut

5 dates, chopped (I like Rancho Meladuco)

2 tablespoons hemp hearts

3 tablespoons organic maple syrup

½ teaspoon ground cinnamon

¼ teaspoon kosher salt, or sub JF Spicy Salt

2 tablespoons psyllium husk powder

½ cup (85 g) semisweet chocolate chips (I like Guittard coconut-sugar chips)

PROCESS

1 Preheat the oven to 375°F (190°C). Line a 9 by 12-inch (23 cm by 30.5 cm) baking sheet with aluminum foil. In a large bowl, combine the pumpkin seeds, sunflower seeds, almonds, coconut, dates, hemp hearts, maple syrup, cinnamon, and salt. Put the psyllium husk powder in a medium bowl and stream in 1 cup (240 ml) warm water with one hand while whisking constantly with the other until a loose paste forms. Add the psyllium husk paste to the dry ingredients and, using a rubber spatula, mix into a uniform dough. Add the chocolate chips and mix to evenly distribute.

2 Using a rubber spatula, spread the dough evenly onto the lined baking sheet. The easiest way to ensure that the dough is uniformly spread is to lay a sheet of parchment on top of the dough and press down with the back of another 9 by 12-inch (23 by 30.5 cm) baking sheet. Bake until golden brown and crisp, 35 to 40 minutes.

3 Let sit until cool enough to handle. Pull the bars from the pan using the bottom sheet of parchment and move them to a cutting board. If needed, use a large chef's knife to trim the edges on all sides to create even, sharp edges. Cut into 2½ by 1-inch (6 by 2.5 cm) bars. Let the bars cool completely. Store in an airtight container at room temperature for up to 7 days.

Cauliflower Hash Rancheros

This one can be a hearty breakfast for two or a great group brunch for four. Feel free to scramble the eggs if fried isn't your style. The real beauty of this recipe is that it can be used as an "anytime" meal—it's one of my favorite "girl dinners" if I'm alone in the house. Wrap the runny eggs and the hash in a cassava tortilla for an incredible breakfast burrito to take on the go. The cauliflower rice gives this hash an earthy, grain-like vibe (you will be making a ton of cauliflower rice if you start making the recipes in this book); it stores well in the fridge and works with almost any protein. It's my favorite "filler/filling" side. It fills you up exactly the same and gives you the same satisfaction as regular rice or quinoa. **SERVES 4**

INGREDIENTS

2 tablespoons olive oil, plus more for finishing

1 small yellow onion (4 ounces/115 g), diced

1 clove garlic, minced

1 (24-ounce/910 g) bag frozen cauliflower rice

2 teaspoons chili powder

½ teaspoon onion powder

½ teaspoon smoked paprika

1 teaspoon ground cumin

1 teaspoon dried oregano

1 teaspoon kosher salt, or sub JF Spicy Salt, plus more to taste

2 tablespoons tomato paste

1 tablespoon canned diced green chiles (I like La Preferida)

8 large eggs

8 grain-free tortillas, toasted (I like Coyotas)

Handful chopped fresh cilantro

2 avocados, pitted, peeled, and sliced

Hot sauce, for serving

PROCESS

1 Heat 1 tablespoon of the olive oil in a large skillet over medium-high heat. Add the onions and garlic and cook until softened, about 2 minutes. Add the cauliflower rice and season with the chili powder, onion powder, smoked paprika, cumin, oregano, salt, and tomato paste. Using a spatula or large wooden spoon, mix until the cauliflower is thoroughly coated in the spices. Cook for 12 to 15 minutes, turning at 3- to 5-minute intervals, until the cauliflower is charred. Stir in the chiles and adjust the salt to taste. Reduce the heat to low while you prepare the eggs.

2 In another skillet, working in batches as necessary, add the remaining 1 tablespoon olive oil and fry the eggs over medium heat for about 3 minutes, keeping the yolks runny. Place two toasted, grain-free tortillas on each plate and build up: add a scoop of the cauliflower hash, then a fried egg, a sprinkle of cilantro, avocado slices, and a squeeze of hot sauce. Finish with a drizzle of olive oil.

California Toast

You can take the girl out of California, but you can't take the California out of the girl. I was a vegetarian for the better part of high school and college (at least I was self-aware enough to know I felt better eating less meat). My go-to for any lunch was a sandwich filled with alfalfa sprouts and avocado with a drizzle of Italian dressing. My miss was the giant sub roll I used to eat it on, loaded with pepper Jack cheese.

This updated version gives me all the satisfaction of that veggie sub without the gluten and dairy bloat. I eat one of these a week, if not more, when I can source fresh alfalfa sprouts in downtown NYC. Not as easy as you would expect. Why alfalfa sprouts, you say? Because they give this sandwich an earthy crunch you cannot find with any other sprout or vegetable. They are California to the core, in my opinion, and a necessary flavor component here. They are also a great source of antioxidants, have been shown to reduce cholesterol, and have been said to help with some symptoms of menopause, such as hot flashes and night sweats. (I sometimes eat half a package at once, lol.) **MAKES 1 TOAST**

INGREDIENTS

½ avocado

1 tablespoon fresh lemon juice

Drizzle of olive oil

⅛ teaspoon kosher salt, or sub JF Spicy Salt, plus more to taste

⅛ teaspoon garlic powder

⅛ teaspoon onion powder

¼ teaspoon Korean red pepper flakes (gochugaru)

Crushed red pepper (if you like it spicy; optional)

Freshly cracked black pepper

1 slice of bread or grain-free bread, toasted

1 deli slice cheddar cheese or plant-based cheddar (I like Violife)

2 to 3 thin slices red onion

2 to 3 slices tomato

¼ cup (12 g) alfalfa sprouts

Drizzle of Simple Mustard Vinaigrette (page 118)

PROCESS

1 In a small bowl, mash together the avocado, lemon juice, and drizzle of olive oil. Season with the salt, garlic powder, onion powder, Korean red pepper flakes, crushed red pepper (if using), and fresh cracked black pepper.

2 Top the toast with the cheddar. Spread the avocado mixture evenly on the cheddar, then top with the onions, tomato, and a heaping pile of sprouts. Season with salt (or sub JF Spicy Salt) and freshly cracked black pepper. Finish with the mustard vinaigrette.

Zesty Lime Rice

This simple cilantro-lime rice is a perfect dupe for my kids' fast-casual takeout favorite. So good and loved by kids and adults alike—just pair with any protein of your choice. It's rice but better.

SERVES 4 TO 6

INGREDIENTS

1 bay leaf

2 cups (370 g) long-grain white rice, rinsed until the water runs clear and drained

Kosher salt, or sub JF Spicy Salt

¼ cup chopped fresh cilantro

2 tablespoons fresh lemon juice (from 1 lemon)

Zest of 1 lime (about 1 teaspoon)

2 tablespoons fresh lime juice (from 1 to 2 limes)

PROCESS

1 In a 7-quart (6.5 liter) pot over high heat, bring 2 quarts (2 liters) water and the bay leaf to a boil. Stir in the rice and a generous pinch of salt. Reduce the heat to medium and cook uncovered until the rice is cooked through, 10 to 12 minutes.

2 Drain the rice and return to the same pot. Cook over very low heat, stirring constantly, until excess water has evaporated, about 1 minute. Fluff the rice with a fork. Mix in the cilantro, lemon juice, and lime zest and juice. Taste and adjust the salt.

Cauliflower Taco Rice

Turns out, all of us want rice but don't want the rice. This is one of my most requested recipes. Zhuzh it up however you please with your favorite toppings, accompaniments, and protein. This will be on constant rotation in your house and can be used in the A.M. and P.M. for many recipes. I have a specific way of cooking my cauliflower rice so it's perfect every time, never soggy. The key, in my opinion, is FROZEN cauliflower rice. By cooking it from frozen, thrown straight into a hot pan containing hot oil and whatever sauté starter veg you want (e.g., garlic and onion), the result is perfect rice every time. I also always say "leave it alone"—meaning, let it cook. Stop poking and stirring it as if that will make the process happen faster. Let the liquid absorb—you can stir it at three-minute intervals—and then the cauliflower rice will char. Keep the heat between medium and medium-high to get the right char; you can turn it down once the rice starts to brown. I also like to throw in a bit more oil near the end to help it brown. **SERVES 2 TO 4**

INGREDIENTS

1 tablespoon avocado oil

1 clove garlic, minced

1 small white onion (about 4 ounces/115 g), chopped

1 bag (12 ounces/240 g) frozen cauliflower rice

1 tablespoon chili powder

1 teaspoon ground cumin

½ teaspoon dried oregano

Kosher salt, or sub JF Spicy Salt, and freshly cracked black pepper

1 tablespoon concentrated tomato paste

1 cup (240 ml) vegetable stock

Handful fresh cilantro, leaves and tender stems, chopped

PROCESS

1. In a large skillet, heat the avocado oil over medium heat. Add the garlic and onion and sauté until softened, 1 to 3 minutes. Add the cauliflower rice. As it cooks down, season with the chili powder, cumin, oregano, salt, and freshly cracked black pepper. Add the tomato paste and vegetable broth. Cook, stirring occasionally, until the stock has mostly evaporated, about 10 minutes. Taste and adjust for salt and pepper. Stir in the cilantro.

2. Serve as the base of a hearty taco salad, over chips for nachos, or in tacos with toppings.

"I Miss Bar Food" Buffalo Cauliflower

Since changing my style of eating, I've missed being able to indulge in bar foods and appetizers. So I wanted to re-create some that felt similarly satisfying but with a healthier twist. These are basically cauliflower "nuggets" that deliver the same satisfying, crispy vibe as Buffalo chicken wings. The Buffalo flavor here is not too spicy, but you can amp up the hotness by adding more sauce and extra hot sauce. And coated cauliflower happens to be the perfect vehicle for those flavors since it absorbs all the extra sauce. The florets are coated in a wet batter that gets crispy in the oven and gives off that bar wings vibe. These make for a perfect topping for any salad or a fun spicy side with chicken, seafood, or steak. You can serve over a salad (see below for my favorite to pair with them) or alone as a fun appetizer, with celery and carrots and some extra dipping sauce and JF Vegan ranch if you have it handy. **SERVES 2 TO 4**

INGREDIENTS

For the cauliflower nuggets

- 1 small head cauliflower (1½ pounds/680 g)
- 1 large egg
- ½ cup avocado oil
- 1 teaspoon Dijon mustard
- 1½ teaspoons kosher salt, or sub JF Spicy salt
- ¾ cup (180 ml) cassava flour, plus more as needed
- ½ teaspoon onion powder
- ½ teaspoon garlic powder
- ½ teaspoon paprika
- ⅛ teaspoon ground turmeric
- 1 teaspoon dried thyme
- 1 tablespoon nutritional yeast (optional)
- ¾ cup (180 ml) Buffalo sauce or barbecue sauce, plus more for serving (The New Primal and Primal Kitchen make some great clean options)

For the salad

- 2 heads romaine lettuce, finely chopped
- 1 avocado, peeled, pitted, and diced
- ¼ cup (30 g) chopped red onion
- ¼ cup (35 g) crumbled queso fresco or plant-based cheese
- ¼ cup (45 g) chopped fresh chives
- Simple Mustard Vinaigrette (page 118)
- Mayo-Free Vegan Ranch (page 116)
- Kosher salt and freshly cracked black pepper

(recipe continues)

PROCESS

Make the cauliflower nuggets

1 Preheat the oven to 425°F (220°C). Line a large baking sheet with aluminum foil. Cut the cauliflower into small florets.

2 In a large bowl, whisk together the egg, avocado oil, mustard, and salt. Add the cassava flour, onion powder, garlic powder, paprika, turmeric, thyme, and nutritional yeast, if using. Whisk to form a batter the consistency of pancake batter. If it's too thin, whisk in a few more teaspoons of cassava flour at a time. If it's too thick, add a few teaspoons of water to loosen it up.

3 Add the cauliflower florets to the large bowl with the batter and toss to coat well. Place the florets on the prepared baking sheet in a single layer and bake for 20 minutes, or until the crust is golden brown.

4 Remove the cauliflower from the oven. Using a pastry brush, brush the baked florets with half of the buffalo or barbecue sauce, then return to the oven for another 12 to 15 minutes, until they start to brown. Remove from the oven and brush with the remaining sauce. Allow to cool slightly before assembling the salad.

Make the salad

5 In a large bowl, combine the lettuce, avocado, red onion, queso fresco, chives, and buffalo cauliflower. Dress with mustard vinaigrette, mayo-free ranch, and additional buffalo or barbecue sauce as desired. Season with salt and freshly cracked black pepper.

Warm and Spicy Shrimp, Mango, and Avocado Salad

OK, a few tips here about shrimp. And all seafood. Always buy wild. NO excuses. I also prefer frozen wild shrimp to fresh. Why? They are frozen in a specific environment and don't stink up the house like when you get a not-so-fresh "fresh" batch at the grocery store. Frozen wild shrimp are my jam. They are always in the freezer, ready to go when the mood hits, and they defrost super-fast (faster than any other protein). Here's the trick: Pull out the amount of shrimp you want to cook and place them in a bowl large enough to cover the shrimp in water. Using cool water, cover the shrimp. Change the water every 3 to 5 minutes, and they will be defrosted in no time. The pro tip here is to pour off the water as soon as it's freezing cold and replace it with reg temp. Lay the shrimp on a paper towel to dry, and pat dry. They take no time and are a great protein choice. I don't eat them that often (every two weeks or so), so I don't worry about the cholesterol levels.

This is the easiest shrimp recipe you will ever make. Perfect for hot summer nights, as it can be served at room temperature and can withstand the wait at the buffet. The fresh and sweet mango, avocado, and corn combination with the bite from the fresh jalapeño makes this the ultimate summer barbecue side. Feel free to serve it over finely chopped romaine or arugula to make it a "leafy" salad for a larger crowd. This also makes for a great single-serve appetizer bite or a low-stress dinner party starter served in individual cups that looks impressive without the stress of keeping it hot. **SERVES 4**

(recipe continues)

INGREDIENTS

2 tablespoons olive oil

2 cloves garlic, minced

1 bag (10 ounces/280 g) frozen sweet corn kernels, thawed

1 pound (455 g) large wild shrimp, shelled and deveined

¼ teaspoon kosher salt, or sub JF Spicy Salt, plus more to taste

Freshly cracked black pepper

2 tablespoons minced roasted red pepper

Jalapeño chile, seeded and finely chopped

½ cup (75 g) chopped red onion

1 firm medium mango (8 ounces/225 g), peeled, pitted, and chopped

1 avocado, pitted, peeled, and chopped

¼ cup chopped fresh cilantro

Crushed red pepper

¼ cup (60 ml) Simple Mustard Vinaigrette (page 118)

2 tablespoons fresh lemon juice

PROCESS

1 Heat the olive oil and garlic in a large skillet over medium-high heat. Cook until the garlic is aromatic and softened, about 30 seconds. Add the corn and sauté, stirring occasionally, until the kernels are slightly charred, about 6 minutes. Add the shrimp and season with the salt and freshly cracked black pepper to taste. Sauté for about 1½ minutes, until the shrimp are opaque throughout. Remove from the heat and place the contents of the pan in a large bowl. Allow to cool slightly.

2 Add the vinaigrette to the bowl and toss to coat the shrimp. Let sit for a few minutes for the shrimp and corn to absorb the dressing. Add the roasted red pepper, jalapeño, red onion, mango, avocado, cilantro, and crushed red pepper to taste. Toss to combine. Taste and adjust the seasoning. Serve immediately at room temperature.

Grain-Free Crab Cakes

These crab cakes are so freakin' good you wouldn't realize they are grain-free and dairy-free. Make mini bite-size versions for cocktail parties or large patties as an entrée for a protein-packed different dinner that will become one of your favorites. I prefer the canned pasteurized wild crabmeat you can purchase at most Whole Foods Markets (in the tinned fish section) or from most fishmongers (you can also buy them at Essex Market in NYC). Or get ready for this . . . yet another random pro tip: Order it from Amazon! Get the Crown Prince fancy white lump crabmeat that comes in a pack of two 6-ounce (170 g) cans, so you are never stuck with a fishy-smelling cake, as sometimes happens with the fresh version. Trust me, it works every time—you have perfect chunk meat crab cake perfection.

MAKES 6 TO 8 CRAB CAKES

INGREDIENTS

For the mango and corn salsa

1 mango, pitted, peeled, and diced

1 cup (145 g) fresh corn kernels

¼ cup (30 g) chopped red onion

1 jalapeño chile, seeded and diced

¼ cup (60 ml) chopped fresh cilantro

1 tablespoon olive oil

Kosher salt, or sub JF Spicy Salt

For the cilantro-lime yogurt sauce

½ cup (120 ml) unsweetened coconut yogurt

¼ cup (10 g) chopped fresh cilantro, leaves and tender stems

1 tablespoon fresh lime juice

⅛ teaspoon ground cumin

¼ teaspoon kosher salt, or sub JF Spicy Salt

¼ teaspoon honey or maple syrup

For the crab cakes

¾ cup (70 g) crumbled almond flour crackers (I like Simple Mills)

1 pound (455 g) crabmeat

½ cup (120 ml) plain coconut yogurt (I like Culina)

2 egg yolks

1 tablespoon Dijon mustard

2 tablespoons chopped fresh cilantro, leaves and tender stems

1½ teaspoons Old Bay Seasoning

½ teaspoon kosher salt, or sub JF Spicy Salt

Freshly cracked black pepper

(recipe continues)

PROCESS

1 Preheat the oven to 450°F (230°C). Line a large baking sheet with aluminum foil.

2 Make the mango and corn salsa: In a small bowl, combine the mango, corn, red onion, jalapeño, cilantro, and olive oil. Season with salt to taste.

3 Make the cilantro-lime yogurt sauce: In a blender, combine the coconut yogurt, cilantro, lime juice, ground cumin, salt, and honey and blend until smooth. Taste and adjust the seasoning, if desired.

4 Make the crab cakes: Using a food processor, pulse the grain-free crackers until they reach a breadcrumb-like texture. Set aside. In a large mixing bowl, mix the crabmeat, yogurt, egg yolks, mustard, cilantro, Old Bay, salt, pepper to taste, and crushed crackers until well combined.

5 Drizzle olive oil onto the prepared baking sheet. Using your hands, form the crab mixture into 6 to 8 cakes and place them on the baking sheet. Bake for about 15 minutes, until the cakes are light golden, then flip and bake for another 15 minutes, or until golden brown.

6 Serve the crab cakes topped with the mango and corn salsa with cilantro-lime yogurt sauce on the side.

Summer Yogurt Bowl

This is hands-down my favorite thing to make when I'm not intermittent fasting and want a spicy-sweet breakfast. I always keep ingredients for this in my house and eat it at all hours of the day. I like to pack this one for lunch when I don't want a leafy green salad. Feel free to sub the mango with peaches or pineapple—they are all awesome. Extra olive oil or chili olive oil makes it extra tasty. **SERVES 1**

INGREDIENTS

1 cup (240 ml) plain coconut yogurt (I like Cocojune or Culina)

½ fresh mango, pitted, peeled, and chopped

½ avocado, pitted, peeled, and chopped

¼ jalapeño chile, seeded and thinly sliced

1 tablespoon roughly chopped fresh cilantro

Freshly cracked black pepper

¼ teaspoon kosher salt, or sub JF Spicy Salt

Olive oil, for drizzling

PROCESS

Spoon the yogurt into a bowl. Layer the mango, avocado, jalapeño, cilantro, pepper to taste, and salt on top. Finish with a generous drizzle of olive oil.

Grilled Pizza Tomatoes

My Grilled Pizza Tomatoes are a great use for summer produce—legit so yummy they taste just like pizza! Perfect for summer barbecues or weekend lunches with the fam, they can easily be made dairy-free with a plant-based cheese. Make them inside on your grill pan for a perfect addition to a basic chicken dinner or paired with my Mom's Not Lazy, Lazy Chicken (page 167). No grill pan? Char them under the broiler for a similar effect, turning a few times to get the desired char. **SERVES 4 TO 6**

INGREDIENTS

4 beefsteak tomatoes, halved

2 tablespoons extra-virgin olive oil

½ shallot, minced

1 tablespoon minced fresh thyme

⅛ teaspoon kosher salt, or sub JF Spicy Salt, plus more to taste

¼ cup (25 g) Parmesan cheese or plant-based Parmesan (I like Violife)

PROCESS

1 Brush your halved tomatoes with olive oil and arrange them face sides up on the grill. As the bottoms cook, sprinkle them with the minced shallot, thyme, and salt.

2 Flip to the other side for an even grill, then turn back to face sides up and sprinkle over the Parmesan. Turn face down to allow the cheese to melt, then repeat a second time for an extra layer of cheese. Season with additional salt and enjoy!

Universal Protein Meatballs

These super-simple baked meatballs are perfect when you need a quick protein fix. As I age, I've been much more aware of "getting my protein in" to maintain muscle mass and energy levels throughout the day. So always having these on hand is important in my house these days. I honestly snack on these cold out of the fridge and don't even bother to heat them up—they are that good. You can use any form of ground meat you want. My personal favorites are chicken or turkey. I like to double the recipe so I can grab them on the regular out of the fridge as an alternative to snacking on a meat stick or hard-boiled egg.

MAKES ABOUT 12 MEATBALLS

INGREDIENTS

1 tablespoon olive oil

¼ cup (30 g) chopped yellow onion

3 cloves garlic, minced

1 pound (455 g) ground chicken, turkey, or grass-fed beef (I like 80/20% ground beef)

1 large egg

1 teaspoon kosher salt, or sub JF Spicy Salt, plus more for sprinkling

½ teaspoon onion powder

½ teaspoon garlic powder

½ teaspoon freshly cracked black pepper

PROCESS

1. Preheat the oven to 350°F (175°C). Line a large baking sheet with aluminum foil and lightly spray with olive or avocado oil. In a small skillet, heat the olive oil over medium heat. Add the onion and sauté for 2 minutes, then add the garlic and cook, tossing often, until the onions are translucent, about 3 minutes. Remove from the heat and let cool.
2. In a large bowl, combine your ground meat of choice and the egg. Season with the salt, onion powder, garlic powder, and pepper. Add the cooled onion and garlic and mix to combine. Do not overmix or the meatballs will be tough.
3. Using your hands, roll out twelve roughly 1-inch (2.5 cm) meatballs. Place the meatballs onto the lined baking sheet and spray them lightly with some olive or avocado oil spray. Sprinkle with salt and bake for 10 to 12 minutes, until the interior temperature reads 165°F (75°C). It's normal for the meatballs to release some foggy liquid. If you want golden crust on the meatballs, finish them under the broiler for about 5 minutes.
4. You can store cooled meatballs in an airtight container for up to 3 days. They won't make it that long, though, trust me. I eat them plain constantly as a snack out of the container. Serve them with tomato sauce, pesto, or even cold, cut up over a salad.

SALADS &

LUNCH IDEAS

The "I'll Have What She's Having" Salad

Craig's is such an iconic Hollywood institution, known for celebrity sightings and classic Italian food. I've been lucky to have built a friendship with Craig over many years of visits. One night, after a few martinis, I pitched the idea for this salad to him. I had always longed for a clean, anti-inflammatory salad you could order in a restaurant or online for delivery but never had any luck. So we put our brains together and had the best time collaborating. In the late summer of 2022, we launched this salad with a huge response from our combined communities in LA. It was so successful it ran for about six months. Evidently more people were looking for the same thing. I thought it was fitting to include it in this cookbook so you can make it at home on your own. Thank you again, Craig, for making this happen. It was a pinnacle food moment for me that gave me the confidence to keep being creative in the kitchen.

Side note: This salad was served finely chopped, which is my preferred way to eat salads. The fine dice is essential because of the abundance of components. I feel if it's chopped finely, an even ratio in each bite is more likely, resulting in a more satisfying salad.

SERVES 2 TO 4

INGREDIENTS

1 large sweet potato (8 ounces/225 g), peeled and diced

Olive oil, for drizzling

Kosher salt, or sub JF Spicy Salt

2 heads romaine, chopped

1 cup (20 g) baby arugula

2 small Persian cucumbers

¼ cup (30 g) chopped red onion

1 avocado, peeled, pitted, and chopped

½ cup (85 g) chopped cooked beets

¼ cup (35 g) fresh pomegranate seeds

¼ cup (35 g) raw sunflower seeds

Simple Mustard Vinaigrette (page 118)

PROCESS

1 Preheat the oven to 400°F (205°C). Line a baking sheet with aluminum foil. Toss the sweet potatoes with a drizzle of olive oil and salt to taste. Roast for about 20 minutes, until tender. Remove from the oven and cool completely.

2 In a large bowl, toss the romaine, arugula, cucumbers, red onion, avocado, the roasted sweet potato, beets, pomegranate seeds, and sunflower seeds. Dress with mustard vinaigrette to coat and finish with a sprinkle of salt.

An "Egg Salad I Can Stomach" Egg Salad

I love eggs, but I despise mayo and the egg salad you might find at delis and grocery stores that's made with it. This version is free of mayo and egg yolks but truly eats like an egg salad. The creaminess of the avocado helps bind all the ingredients together. Topping some bread with it might seem like the right move here, but my favorite way to eat this is to scoop it on some tortilla chips. For a vinegary kick, top it with some hot sauce. **SERVES 2 TO 4**

INGREDIENTS

5 large hard-boiled eggs, yolks removed, whites chopped

⅓ cup (35 g) chopped red onion

⅓ cup (35 g) chopped celery

½ avocado, peeled, pitted, and chopped

2 radishes, trimmed and chopped

1½ teaspoons chopped Fresno chile

¼ teaspoon kosher salt, or sub JF salt of your choice, plus more to taste

¼ teaspoon garlic powder

1 tablespoon chopped fresh cilantro

Tortilla chips and hot sauce, for serving

PROCESS

In a medium bowl, combine the egg whites, red onion, celery, avocado, radish, and chile and lightly mix together—you want the salad to stay chunky, not get mushy. Season with the salt and garlic powder. Top with the cilantro. Serve with tortilla chips and hot sauce.

The Veginator

Veggies have always been more my vibe than meat, so I was vegetarian for most of my young adult life. An earlier version of this sandwich was piled high with pepper Jack cheese on a chewy baguette, both of which you can opt for instead of the dairy- and grain-free alternatives featured in this recipe. The updated Veginator leans on avocado mash amped up by my simple mustard vinaigrette and the smoke of the Gouda, for a creamy companion to the shiitake bacon. **SERVES 1**

INGREDIENTS

For the vegan shiitake bacon

½ teaspoon olive oil

8 ounces (225 g) sliced shiitake mushrooms

1 tablespoon coconut aminos or tamari

1½ teaspoons maple syrup

1 teaspoon liquid smoke

1 teaspoon smoked paprika

½ teaspoon kosher salt, or sub JF Spicy Salt

Freshly cracked black pepper

JF Avocado Mash and Assembly

½ avocado

Kosher salt, or sub JF salt of your choice

1 tablespoon Simple Mustard Vinaigrette (page 118), plus more to taste

2 teaspoons Dijon mustard

1 grain-free bread, sliced and toasted (I like AWG Bakery Rosemary or Everything breads)

1 slice plant-based smoked Gouda cheese, cut in half (I like 365)

1 tablespoon chopped hot cherry peppers (I like Jeff's Garden)

¼ cup (12 g) alfalfa sprouts

PROCESS

Make the vegan shiitake bacon

Warm the olive oil in a large skillet over medium-high heat. Add the mushrooms, coconut aminos, maple syrup, liquid smoke, and paprika and toss to coat the mushrooms evenly. Season with salt and freshly cracked black pepper to taste. Sauté for about 7 minutes, until the mushrooms brown and crisp slightly on the edges but still retain some bite. Remove to a plate to cool completely before assembly.

Make the avocado mash

In a small bowl, lightly mash the avocado with the back of a fork. Season with salt and dress with mustard vinaigrette as desired.

Assemble the sandwich

Spread the mustard on one half of the baguette. Layer on the Gouda, cherry peppers, avocado mash, shiitake bacon, and sprouts, then top with the second half of the baguette.

Mayo-Free Chicken Salad

Mayo and I have never been friends, so needless to say, any mayo-based salad is a *no* for me. I've always been put off by the beige, amorphous, mayo-ladened gloop at delis and grocery stores labeled "chicken salad." I yearned for a fresher, brighter, and, of course, mayo-free version, which is what inspired this recipe. A few hours in the slow cooker or a Dutch oven yields perfectly shreddable chicken breasts (or a rotisserie chicken if you're pressed for time). Combined with celery, red onion, cilantro, and a generous portion of my simple mustard vinaigrette (page 118), the chicken turns into the salad I used to dream of. Scoop it on top of a bowl of greens, tuck it inside a lettuce wrap (my personal favorite), or serve it as a melt on toast topped with your favorite cheese. **SERVES 4 TO 6**

INGREDIENTS

- JF Crock-Pot Chicken, shredded (at right), or 2 cups (390 g) shredded rotisserie chicken
- ½ cup (50 g) chopped celery
- ¼ cup (10 g) chopped fresh cilantro
- ¼ cup (30 g) chopped red onion
- ¼ cup (60 ml) Simple Mustard Vinaigrette (page 118)
- ¼ teaspoon kosher salt or sub JF Spicy Salt, plus more to taste

PROCESS

Assemble the salad

In a large bowl, mix together the shredded chicken, celery, cilantro, red onion, vinaigrette, and salt. Adjust the salt to taste and mix until thoroughly combined. Enjoy immediately or store in an airtight container in the fridge for up to 2 days.

JF Crock-Pot Chicken

- 3 to 4 boneless, skinless chicken breasts (about 2⅓ pounds/1 kg)
- 2 teaspoons garlic powder
- 2 teaspoons onion powder
- 1 teaspoon smoked paprika
- 1 teaspoon kosher salt, or sub JF Spicy Salt
- ½ teaspoon freshly cracked black pepper
- 2 cups (480 ml) chicken broth (I like Bonafide low-sodium)

1 Put the chicken breasts in a slow cooker and add the garlic powder, onion powder, paprika, salt, and pepper. Toss using tongs until the chicken is evenly coated with the seasonings. Or preheat the oven to 250°F (120°C) and toss the chicken with the seasonings in a Dutch oven or other heavy-bottomed pot with a lid.

2. Pour the chicken broth over the breasts, ensuring the breasts are fully submerged. Set the slow cooker on High and cook for 2 to 3 hours, or on Low for 3 to 4 hours. If using the oven, cover the Dutch oven and cook for 2 to 2½ hours. The chicken is done when firm but tender and opaque and the internal temperature reaches 165°F (75°C).
3. Pull the chicken out of the broth and allow to cool slightly (the leftover broth makes for an excellent base for noodle soup). Shred with a fork and set aside for the salad assembly.

"Tastes Like Chicken" Mushroom Salad with Vegan Ranch

I promise there's a good reason behind the name of this recipe. Oyster mushrooms have lots of thin surface area that, when roasted in a hot oven, turn satisfyingly crispy. Add in some homemade poultry seasoning and you have mushrooms that taste like chicken! These are fantastic atop a big bowl of greens and veggies, but if you aren't in the mood for a salad, eat them as an appetizer dipped in vegan ranch (page 116) or as a side for chicken or steak.

SERVES 4 TO 6

INGREDIENTS

1 head romaine, chopped

2 cups (200 g) chopped frisée

2 Persian cucumbers, chopped

⅔ cup (85 g) peeled and chopped jicama

3 radishes, chopped

¼ cup (30 g) chopped red onion

½ avocado, pitted, peeled, and chopped (optional)

¼ cup (60 ml) Mayo-Free Vegan Ranch (page 116), plus more to taste

1 recipe Roasted Oyster Mushrooms (see below)

¼ cup (35 g) raw sunflower seeds

2 tablespoons minced fresh chives

¼ cup (13 g) chopped fresh flat-leaf parsley

Kosher salt, or sub JF Spicy Salt, and freshly cracked black pepper

PROCESS

In a large bowl, combine the romaine, frisée, cucumbers, jicama, radishes, red onion, and avocado (if using). Add the dairy-free ranch, plus more if desired, and toss thoroughly to coat. Arrange the roasted oyster mushrooms on top while still warm, and top with the sunflower seeds. Finish with the chives and parsley. Season with salt and freshly cracked pepper to taste.

Roasted Oyster Mushrooms

8 ounces (225 g) oyster mushrooms

½ teaspoon chopped fresh rosemary or dried rosemary

½ teaspoon chopped fresh thyme or dried thyme

½ teaspoon onion powder

½ teaspoon garlic powder

¼ teaspoon smoked paprika

Olive oil

¼ teaspoon kosher salt, or sub JF Spicy Salt

Freshly cracked black pepper

1. Preheat the oven to 375°F (190°C). Line a baking sheet with aluminum foil and lightly drizzle with olive oil.
2. In a large bowl, combine the oyster mushrooms, rosemary, thyme, onion powder, garlic powder, smoked paprika, and a drizzle of olive oil (be sure not to oversaturate them with oil). Mix well until the mushrooms are evenly coated in seasoning.
3. Spread out the mushrooms on the prepared baking sheet. Season with salt and black pepper, tossing to coat. Roast until browned and crisp, about 20 minutes.

"Classic" Tuna, Spa Style

I could never eat tuna salads growing up because of my aversion to mayonnaise. So I created a version that uses my Simple Mustard Vinaigrette (page 118) instead of mayo. This is my take on the traditional tuna salad you normally find at delis and grocery stores. It's so delicious as a tuna melt, over salads, or enjoyed completely on its own! Or modify this simple base to create your new favorite lunch—I included some of my favorite remixes of this recipe below.

SERVES 4

INGREDIENTS

- 2 cans (5 ounces/140 g each) tuna packed in olive oil (I like Wild Planet low-sodium albacore), drained
- 1 tablespoon spicy brown mustard
- 3 tablespoons Simple Mustard Vinaigrette (page 118)
- ⅓ cup (75 g) chopped pickles (I like Grillo's)
- ¼ cup (30 g) chopped white onion
- ⅓ cup (45 g) chopped celery
- ¼ teaspoon freshly cracked black pepper
- Kosher salt, or sub JF Spicy Salt

PROCESS

Put the drained tuna in a large bowl and flake it as finely as possible using the back of a fork. Add the spicy brown mustard and the mustard vinaigrette and mash to combine. Fold in the pickles, onion, and celery and season with the freshly cracked black pepper and salt to taste. Eat immediately or store in an airtight container in the fridge for up to 2 days. I love to wrap mine, as shown here, in Avocado Oil Gimmie seaweed sheets with avocado and hot sauce.

My Favorite Twists:

SPICY TUNA: Omit the pickles and celery and mix in 2 tablespoons finely chopped jalapeño, ¼ cup (10 g) finely chopped fresh cilantro, plus hot sauce of your choice to taste (I like Tia Lupita Classic or Siete Jalapeño Botano).

CRUNCHY TUNA: Omit the pickles and add ⅓ cup (25 g) finely chopped green cabbage and 2 tablespoons chopped pepperoncini.

Italian Sub-Inspired Tuna

Two things: First, I've never met a pepperoncini I didn't like; and second, my favorite food is a perfectly executed sub sandwich—especially one with tuna. This salad turns my favorite sub into lighter fare that comes together faster than spelling "pepperoncini." The briny peppers combined with the heat of Calabrian chiles, and the bite of white onions, transform a humble can of tuna into a salad you'll keep going back to. Take this to work or pack it for the beach over the summer. I promise you it never disappoints. **SERVES 4 TO 6**

INGREDIENTS

2 cans (4 ounces/115 g each) tuna packed in olive oil (preferably low-sodium)

2 tablespoons Dijon mustard

3 tablespoons Simple Mustard Vinaigrette (page 118)

1 tablespoon chopped Calabrian peppers or cherry peppers (about 3 whole peppers)

2 tablespoons chopped pickled pepperoncini

1 small white onion (4 ounces/115 g), finely diced

⅛ teaspoon onion powder

¼ teaspoon garlic powder

½ teaspoon Korean red pepper flakes (gochujang)

1 tablespoon fresh lemon juice

Kosher salt, or sub JF Spicy Salt

¼ cup (13 g) chopped fresh flat-leaf parsley

PROCESS

Put the drained tuna in a large bowl and flake using the back of a fork until no clumps remain. Add the mustard, mustard vinaigrette, Calabrian peppers, pepperoncini, and onion. Using a fork, mix until thoroughly combined. Season with the onion powder, garlic powder, red pepper flakes, lemon juice, and salt to taste. Top with the fresh flat-leaf parsley. Store leftovers in an airtight container for up to 2 days.

The Bomb Salad

There isn't much to this one. But it truly is "the bomb." There is something about the creaminess of the vegan feta and the mild olives and the bite of the radicchio with red onion and radish that makes this my favorite "green" salad. I should call this the "base salad," as I use it for many of my packed lunches for work, topped with spa-style tuna (page 92) or eat it for dinner with chicken or shrimp. Triple the yield for a casual potluck or dinner party—everyone will be asking for the recipe. **SERVES 2 TO 4**

INGREDIENTS

3 tablespoons olive oil

Juice of 1 lemon (about 3 tablespoons)

2 teaspoons honey

Kosher salt, or sub JF Spicy Salt, and freshly cracked black pepper

1 head romaine, chopped

1 head butter lettuce, chopped

1 radicchio (8 ounces/225 g), chopped

5 radishes, thinly sliced

⅔ cup (240 g) Castelvetrano olives, pitted and sliced (I prefer Frescatrano by Divina)

3 Persian cucumbers, chopped

⅓ cup (35 g) chopped red onion

¼ cup (25 g) chopped pickled pepperoncini

½ avocado, peeled, pitted, and diced

Handful chopped fresh cilantro, dill, or both

⅓ cup (40 g) goat cheese or plant-based vegan feta cheese (I like Violife)

PROCESS

1 In a large bowl, whisk the olive oil, lemon juice, honey, salt and freshly cracked black pepper to taste until well combined. Taste and adjust for salt and pepper.

2 Combine the romaine and butter lettuces, radicchio, radishes, olives, cucumber, red onion, pepperoncini, avocado, and herbs in a large bowl and toss until well coated with the dressing. Top with the goat cheese and season with more salt and black pepper, if desired.

Mayo-Free Herby Green Goddess Tuna

This is not your basic tuna recipe. This mayo-free tuna is reminiscent of an "herb" green goddess dressing. It's amazing over a finely chopped salad of romaine, cucumbers, and sliced red onion. Throw it into a large cassava tortilla for a perfect lunch wrap with an insane amount of flavor. I also love this scooped up in olive oil potato chips.

SERVES 2 TO 4

INGREDIENTS

2 cans (4 ounces/115 g each) low-sodium tuna packed in olive oil, drained

2 tablespoons Simple Mustard Vinaigrette (page 118)

¼ cup (60 ml) chopped yellow onion

1 clove garlic, minced

1 small shallot, finely chopped

1 jalapeño chile, seeded and finely chopped

1 tablespoon chopped fresh flat-leaf parsley

1 tablespoon chopped fresh chives

1 tablespoon chopped fresh cilantro

1 tablespoon chopped fresh dill

½ teaspoon lemon zest

2 tablespoons fresh lemon juice

Kosher salt, or sub JF salt of your choice, and freshly cracked black pepper

PROCESS

In a large bowl, combine the drained tuna and vinaigrette. Using the back of a fork, flake the tuna really well—you're basically going to mush it. (I prefer the term "finely flaked.") Add the onion, garlic, shallot, jalapeño, parsley, chives, cilantro, dill, lemon zest and juice, and salt and freshly cracked black pepper to taste; stir to combine. Taste and adjust the salt and pepper as desired. Store in an airtight container in the refrigerator for up to 2 days.

NYC × LA Chopped Salad

Anyone who's from the Westside of LA knows the origin of this salad. It's a long-standing staple among the locals and an anchor for Kevin and my twenty-five-year-long relationship. We ate at La Scala often when we started dating. I began making my own version of this salad at home, and before we knew it, we were engaged and soon married. There is "engagement chicken" for some, but for Kevin, it's "engagement salad"—I'm convinced my improvement of this salad sealed the deal for us. And twenty-three married years later, he is now making his version of this salad for himself daily (he's a creature of habit), which garnered it the name "Kevin Salad" in our house. I highly recommend feeding your partner a trough of this salad if you want to be left alone for the night. They eat so much they aren't really in the mood for much else . . . lol.

This recipe is meant to be a guide for you to evolve and modify as you please. I've included all of our favorite ingredients and toppings, but, of course, feel free to add whatever else you might crave on a salad. I like to create a "salad bar" in my house and let everyone choose their own adventure. It makes for an interactive meal that's very easy to set up before guests arrive so you can relax once they do.

I try to make sure the salami I use for this salad is Applegate Organics uncured. I stay away from processed meats, with the exception of this salami and my meat sticks. **SERVES 6 TO 8**

(recipe continues)

INGREDIENTS

For the at-home salad bar

1 bag (3 heads) romaine lettuce, finely chopped

1 head iceberg lettuce, finely chopped

12 slices soppressata or Genoa salami, finely chopped

1 cup (110 g) shredded mozzarella or plant-based mozzarella (I like Violife)

1 recipe Marinated Garbanzo Beans (see opposite)

¼ cup (25 g) diced pimiento peppers

2 avocados, peeled, pitted, and chopped

2 English cucumbers, chopped

1 large red or white onion (8 ounces/ 225 g), chopped

½ cup (80 g) chopped pickled pepperoncini

2 large tomatoes (10 to 12 ounces/280 to 340 g each), seeded and chopped

1 cup (225 g) chopped bacon

6 to 8 slices turkey, chopped

2 cups (460 g) chopped grilled chicken

1 cup (240 ml) Simple Mustard Vinaigrette (page 118)

PROCESS

Make the salad bar

Prepare all the ingredients as instructed and set up the salad bar so each person can customize their own salad bowls. I recommend starting with a base of lettuce, cheese, salami, and pimiento peppers (you just want small bits of red throughout, not too much). Toss together with desired toppings along with a drizzle of the mustard vinaigrette.

Marinated Garbanzo Beans

1 can (29 ounces/820 g) garbanzo beans, drained

2 tablespoons Simple Mustard Vinaigrette (page 118)

2 teaspoons dried dill

2 teaspoons dried cilantro

1 teaspoon crushed red pepper

Zest of 1 lemon

1 teaspoon kosher salt, or sub JF Spicy Salt

In a medium bowl, mix together the garbanzo beans, vinaigrette, dried dill, dried cilantro, crushed red pepper, lemon zest, and salt (see Tip). Cover the bowl and let the garbanzo beans marinate in the fridge for at least 2 hours or overnight.

TIP: You can use JF Universal Salt in place of all the seasonings, if you like.

Shiitake Salami Pasta Salad

Since I started my gluten- and grain-free journey, one thing I miss dearly is a big pasta salad. The kind I used to scoop up from the deli section at grocery stores in college. They are so diverse and fun to put together, so I created this recipe that uses grain-free pasta and a few of my favorite jarred and canned items—like roasted red peppers, artichoke hearts, and black olives. There's also what I call shiitake "salami." Yes, shitake salami . . . hear me out. Ever since I made my first batch of shiitake "bacon," I've been obsessed, so here is the "salami" version. Slightly different spices makes for a different faux meat. It's the perfect substitute for any "salty meat" that used to fill my chopped salads. Trust me, the humble fungi can be equally satisfying as salty meat. **SERVES 4 TO 6**

INGREDIENTS

1 box (8 ounces/225 g) grain-free penne, cooked according to package instructions (I like Jovial)

1 recipe JF Shiitake Salami (see opposite)

3 tablespoons drained and chopped roasted red peppers

3 tablespoons chopped fresh chives

½ cup (65 g) peeled and chopped jicama

1 small tomato (4 ounces/115 g), seeded and chopped

⅓ cup (35 g) chopped red onion

⅓ cup (60 g) canned sliced black olives, drained

¼ cup (25 g) chopped pickled pepperoncini

½ cup (130 g) canned artichoke hearts, drained and chopped (I like Native Forest)

Kosher salt, or sub JF Spicy Salt, and freshly cracked black pepper

Simple Mustard Vinaigrette (page 118

PROCESS

Assemble the pasta: In a large bowl, combine the pasta, shiitake salami, roasted red peppers, chives, jicama, tomato, red onion, black olives, pepperoncini, and artichoke hearts. Season with salt and freshly cracked black pepper to taste. Add a generous amount of mustard vinaigrette and toss well to coat.

Shiitake Salami

Olive oil

8 ounces (225 g) sliced shiitake mushrooms

¼ teaspoon dried thyme

¼ teaspoon fennel seeds

¼ teaspoon dried basil

¼ teaspoon dried parsley

¼ teaspoon crushed red pepper

¼ teaspoon garlic powder

¼ teaspoon onion powder

1 tablespoon nutritional yeast

¼ teaspoon kosher salt, or sub JF Spicy Salt

1 Preheat the oven to 400°F (205°C).

2 In a large oven-safe skillet over medium heat, warm a thin layer of olive oil, just enough to cover the base of the pan. Add the mushrooms and cook until they begin to brown slightly, about 3 minutes. Add the thyme, fennel seeds, basil, parsley, crushed red pepper, garlic powder, onion powder, nutritional yeast, and salt. Sauté until the mushrooms begin to crisp around the edges, 3 to 4 minutes. Transfer the skillet to the oven and roast for 15 minutes, or until the mushrooms are dark and crisp. Store leftovers in an airtight container in the refrigerator for up to 2 days.

JF Slaw

In my house we love any kind of crunchy veg. This slaw came from my wanting a non-mayo slaw to go with my brisket, and we've never looked back. In fact, this is the preferred "side salad" in my house. Kevin can dig into this like a trough salad. The lighter the dressing the better, so the flavors of the vegetables come through; it's finished with an extra pinch of salt on top. It's also my go to for crunch in any wrap or taco. **SERVES 2**

INGREDIENTS

4 cups (380 g) thinly shredded green cabbage

½ cup (380 g) thinly shredded red cabbage

¼ cup (30 g) shredded carrots

¼ cup (35 g) finely chopped red onion

¼ cup (10 g) chopped fresh cilantro (optional)

2 tablespoons finely chopped jalapeño chile

3 radishes, cut into matchsticks

¼ cup (60 ml) Simple Mustard Vinaigrette (page 118)

Kosher salt, or sub JF Spicy Salt

PROCESS

In a large bowl, combine the green and red cabbage, carrots, red onion, cilantro, jalapeño, radishes, mustard vinaigrette, and a generous pinch of salt. Mix thoroughly with your hands. Taste and adjust the seasoning.

Mediterranean Garlic Chicken with Grain-Free Cauliflower Tabbouleh

Cauliflower tabbouleh is my answer to all the grains I can no longer eat with my proteins. It's packed with herbs as well as crisped cauliflower rice and crunchy cucumbers and scratches the itch of the bite you get from rice or quinoa. To ensure the cauliflower rice develops all the crispy bits possible, make sure not to mess with it too much while it cooks. Hit it with a generous squeeze of lemon and even some zest, and you'll have lunches for days. You'll never miss the grain here! **SERVE 4 TO 6**

INGREDIENTS

For the garlic chicken

- 3 to 4 boneless chicken breasts (about 2¼ pounds/692 g), cut crosswise into thin slices
- 1 medium shallot, finely chopped
- 4 cloves garlic, minced
- 1 tablespoon chopped fresh parsley
- 1½ teaspoons dried oregano
- 1 teaspoon onion powder
- 1 teaspoon kosher salt, or sub JF Spicy or JF Universal Salt
- 1 teaspoon Korean red pepper flakes (gochujang)
- 1 tablespoon olive oil
- 1 tablespoon fresh lemon juice

For the cauliflower tabbouleh

- 1 tablespoon olive oil
- 1 clove garlic, minced
- ¾ cup (85 g) diced white onion
- 1 bag (12 ounces/340 g) frozen cauliflower rice
- ½ teaspoon kosher salt or, sub JF Spicy or JF Universal Salt
- 5 Persian cucumbers, chopped
- 2 small ripe tomatoes (4 ounces/115 g each), seeded and diced
- ¼ cup (30 g) chopped red onion
- 2 cups (100 g) chopped fresh flat-leaf parsley (about 1 bunch)
- 2 tablespoons minced fresh mint leaves

PROCESS

Marinate the chicken

1 Put the chicken in a large bowl and add the shallot, garlic, parsley, oregano, onion powder, salt, and Korean red pepper flakes. Add a drizzle of olive oil and mix using tongs until the chicken is evenly coated in seasoning. Let the chicken marinate in the fridge for at least 1 hour and up to 1 day.

Make the cauliflower rice

2 Heat the olive oil in a large skillet over medium-high heat. Add the garlic, onion, and cauliflower rice. Mix using a spatula until the cauliflower rice is evenly coated in oil. Cook the cauliflower rice, stirring only every 3 to 4 minutes, for a total of 12 to 15 minutes—you'll want to give it time to cook undisturbed so it can develop crispy bits. Season with salt and let cool.

Assemble the salad

3 Heat 1 tablespoon olive oil in a medium skillet over medium-high heat. Add the chicken and cook, stirring often, until the chicken slices are cooked through but still tender, about 8 minutes. Stir in the lemon juice and remove from the heat.

4 In a large bowl, mix the cooled cauliflower rice, cucumbers, tomatoes, red onion, parsley, and mint. Season with salt to taste. Serve the garlic chicken over the cauliflower tabbouleh. Leftovers work well here as a working lunch as well.

Green Greek Salad

I have had versions of this at many Mediterranean restaurants. But I always felt like I could one-up it by chopping it finer and adding a few extra components. The result, this simple combination of a few fresh ingredients, is perfect with any protein. I always make this when I want a fast, crisp salad in a hurry. It's also great as a side salad for any potluck or group dinner—you can simply triple the recipe. A perpetual hit among adults and kids . . . there are never any leftovers of this one. Sign of a true hit. Going to a potluck or BBQ? Bring this (or the NYC × LA Chopped Salad, page 99). People will talk about it, and you'll always be asked to bring it again. **SERVES 4**

INGREDIENTS

1 head iceberg lettuce, finely chopped

½ cup (25 g) chopped fresh dill

½ large Persian cucumber, seeded and finely diced

½ cup (75 g) crumbled feta or plant-based feta (I like Violife)

2 green onions, halved lengthwise and thinly sliced on the diagonal

½ cup (50 g) chopped pickled pepperoncini

¼ cup (40 g) pitted and chopped Kalamata olives

1 tablespoon fresh lemon juice

½ avocado, peeled, pitted, and chopped (optional)

¼ cup Simple Mustard Vinaigrette, or to taste (page 118)

¼ cup (40 g) sliced fresh jalapeño chiles or 2 tablespoons chopped cherry peppers (optional), if you want it spicy

Kosher salt, or sub JF Spicy Salt, and freshly cracked black pepper

PROCESS

In a large bowl, combine the lettuce, dill, cucumber, feta, green onions, pepperoncini, olives, lemon juice, avocado, vinaigrette, jalapeños, and salt to taste and toss well to mix. Finish with freshly cracked black pepper and more salt as needed and serve.

Sweet and Savory Shrimp and Plantain Salad

I've always been obsessed with plantains. When we lived in SoHo back in the mid-2000s, around the time my son Shane was born, we would frequently order food from a local Mexican restaurant called Lupe's. Kevin would get the chicken, and I would get the plantains, shrimp, and beans. Back then, my beans were smothered in cheese and the plantains were fried in vegetable oil. I may not be able to eat that way anymore, but I still miss that order very much, and that's what inspired this recipe. This salad gives you the best of both worlds—sweet and savory, and no seed oils to leave you swollen and inflamed. You can fry the plantains and cook the shrimp ahead of time to assemble the salad in just a few minutes. You can also substitute the shrimp with Mom's Not-Lazy, Lazy Chicken (page 167). **SERVES 4 TO 6**

INGREDIENTS

For the pan-fried plantains

Olive oil (I like Kyoord), coconut oil, or avocado oil, for frying

2 yellow plantains (8 to 12 ounces/225 to 340 g), peeled and sliced on a bias about ¼ inch (6 mm) thick

Kosher salt, or sub JF Spicy or JF Universal Salt

For the sautéed shrimp

8 ounces (225 g) medium shrimp, peeled and deveined

1 teaspoon Korean red pepper flakes (gochujang)

¼ teaspoon garlic powder

½ teaspoon onion powder

½ teaspoon kosher salt, or sub JF Spicy or JF Universal Salt

Freshly cracked black pepper

Avocado oil or olive oil, for drizzling and frying

For the salad

1 head romaine, chopped

1½ cups (145 g) shredded red cabbage

3 Persian cucumbers, chopped

1 small red onion, finely chopped

4 radishes, thinly sliced

½ cup (70 g) raw sunflower seeds

About 3 tablespoons Simple Mustard Vinaigrette (page 118), or to taste

½ teaspoon kosher salt, or sub JF Spicy or JF Universal Salt, plus more to taste

PROCESS

Fry the plantains

1 Set a wire rack on top of a baking sheet and place a paper towel on top. In a large skillet over medium heat, add just enough olive oil to cover the bottom of the pan. Once the oil is hot, add the plantains evenly in one layer, working in batches if necessary. Fry until the bottoms are browned, 1½ to 2 minutes, then flip. Fry the other side until browned, about 1 minute. Place the plantains on the paper towel set over the wire rack to drain and season with salt. Add additional oil if necessary and repeat the process with the remaining plantains. Clean the skillet.

Sauté the shrimp

2 In a medium bowl, combine the shrimp, red pepper flakes, garlic powder, onion powder, salt, freshly cracked black pepper to taste, and a drizzle of avocado oil. Mix until the shrimp is evenly coated with the seasoning.

3 In a large skillet over medium heat, warm enough avocado oil to coat the bottom, about 1 tablespoon. Once the oil begins to shimmer, add the shrimp and cook for 3 minutes. Flip the shrimp and cook for 2 minutes or so—they are done when they begin to curl and turn pink. Remove the shrimp and set aside on a wire rack or plate to cool completely.

Assemble the salad

4 Chop the cooked shrimp into bite-size pieces. In a large bowl, combine the romaine, red cabbage, cucumbers, radishes, sunflower seeds, shrimp, and plantains. Add the mustard vinaigrette and season with salt.

DIPS, SPREADS & DRESSINGS

Cauliflower Hummus

This is a sick appetizer and is the best sub for regular hummus for a party or snack. I had been craving hummus and decided to make a bean-free cauliflower version. I personally find many legumes inflammatory, so I normally limit them. This hummus is all the dip sans the beans and bloat. Serve this with cucumbers and other vegetables. It's crazy how close to regular hummus this is. Make sure to top with good olive oil and some olives, plus a touch of smoked paprika and salt. **SERVES 2 TO 4**

INGREDIENTS

- 1 large head cauliflower (1½ pounds/680 g), trimmed and cut into florets
- Olive oil, for drizzling
- ¼ cup (60 ml) organic tahini
- 2 cloves garlic
- ¼ teaspoon ground cumin
- ⅛ teaspoon ground coriander
- 2 tablespoons fresh lemon juice
- ½ teaspoon kosher salt, or sub JF Spicy, JF Universal, or JF Curry salt, plus more to taste

For serving

- 1 tablespoon chopped fresh flat-leaf parsley
- 1 lemon, cut into wedges
- ½ teaspoon smoked paprika
- 7 olives

PROCESS

1. Preheat the oven to 450°F (230°C). Line a large baking sheet with aluminum foil. Place the cauliflower florets on the baking sheet and toss with the olive oil. Roast until tender, about 15 minutes. Remove from the oven and let cool slightly.

2. In a blender, combine the cauliflower, tahini, garlic cloves, cumin, coriander, lemon juice, and salt. Blend until smooth. Taste and adjust the seasoning. Serve topped with parsley, a squeeze of lemon, a pinch of smoked paprika, olives, and a drizzle of olive oil and some salt.

Grandma Lulie's Orange Cranberry Sauce

My mother has made this every year since I can remember, and it is a requirement for all Thanksgiving gatherings (as are my aunt Jeanette's pearl onions, but those are for another book). This orange cranberry sauce gives a slight nod to cherry pie filling, but it's cranberry. It's tart and sweet, which makes it the perfect complement to pretty much any protein. I have to make extras for my BFF every year, because she uses it as a sauce for all of her proteins for weeks after the holiday. So try making a big batch at Rosh Hashanah, Yom Kippur, or Christmas too—it's not just for Thanksgiving and turkey. It's incredible on ham and brisket as well. **SERVES 8**

INGREDIENTS

- 3 naval oranges
- 1 quart (2 liters) fresh cranberries, rinsed and dried or frozen, thawed
- 1¼ cups (250 g) granulated sugar or 1¼ cups (240 g) coconut sugar, plus more to taste
- ¼ teaspoon kosher salt

PROCESS

Peel the oranges and trim the pith. Separate them into sections and remove the seeds, then chop. In a small saucepan over medium heat, cook the cranberries, sugar, and salt, stirring and crushing the berries, until the cranberries begin to burst and release their juices. Once all the cranberries have burst open and become soft and jammy, add the orange pieces and continue to cook until the cranberry sauce has thickened. If too tart, add more sugar to taste. Store in an airtight container in the refrigerator for up to 3 days; it also freezes well.

NOTE: *I like to make this a day ahead, so the flavors have a chance to settle and develop overnight.*

Creamy Lemon, Garlic, and Dill Dressing

This is pretty much the only "creamy" dressing I can tolerate. And it's addictive. You might notice there is very little tahini in this cookbook, because I'm not a fan. BUT I'm a fan of this. It's incredible over any grain or warm veggie rice, and even as a dipping sauce for chicken. If you don't normally love dill, this might change your mind. This is a thicker dressing that can be used as a dip as well, for fresh veggies on a veggie platter. **MAKES ABOUT 2½ CUPS (600 ML)**

INGREDIENTS

- 1 cup (120 g) raw cashews
- 1 teaspoon Dijon mustard
- 1 teaspoon kosher salt, or sub JF Spicy Salt
- 2 cloves garlic, germs removed
- 2 tablespoons fresh lemon juice
- 1 cup (50 g) chopped fresh dill, leaves and tender stems
- 1 cup (240 ml) nut milk (I like Three Trees almond milk)
- ¼ teaspoon freshly cracked black pepper

PROCESS

In a small saucepan, soak the cashews in 2 cups (480 ml) water for 30 minutes. Bring to a boil over medium heat, then reduce the heat to low and simmer for 10 to 15 minutes, until the cashews are hydrated and tender.

Drain the cashews and add to a blender along with the mustard, salt, garlic, lemon juice, dill, nut milk, and freshly cracked black pepper. Blend for 3 minutes, or until the dressing is completely smooth with little to no graininess.

Mayo-Free Vegan Ranch

I'm from California, so I consider ranch essential (so is pineapple on pizza). And if you know me, you know I don't do mayo or aioli, so this recipe came early on for me. My ranch recipe has evolved over the years, so now it's completely dairy-free—and just as good. I prefer this as a dipping sauce or drizzled over something rather than using it as a salad dressing. It's also intentionally more herby than the norm. Load it up with dill and flat-leaf parsley.

MAKES ABOUT 1 CUP (240 ML)

INGREDIENTS

1 container (4 to 5 ounces/115 g to 140 g) dairy-free plain yogurt (I like Cocojune)

¼ cup (60 ml) plain unsweetened almond milk (I like Three Trees)

½ teaspoon garlic powder

½ teaspoon onion powder

¼ teaspoon dried dill

⅛ teaspoon freshly cracked black pepper

¼ teaspoon kosher salt or sub JF Spicy Salt

1 tablespoon chopped fresh chives

1 tablespoon chopped fresh flat-leaf parsley

Crushed red pepper

PROCESS

In a medium bowl, whisk together the yogurt, almond milk, garlic powder, onion powder, dried dill, freshly cracked black pepper, salt, chives, parsley, and crushed red pepper to taste. Taste and adjust the seasoning, and serve immediately. This ranch can be kept in the fridge for up to 3 days. Mix well before serving.

Chimichurri

This is easy, bright, and so flavorful. I originally made this when my kids were little and loving lamb chops; I wanted something simple and fresh for the adults to use as a dip for the lamb. But it also goes with pretty much any protein. It's even good on leftover noodles. I put this sh*t on anything.

MAKES ABOUT 2 CUPS (480 ML)

INGREDIENTS

¼ cup (60 ml) olive oil, plus more for sautéing the garlic

4 cloves garlic, minced

1 cup (40 g) loosely packed fresh cilantro leaves

1 cup (50 g) loosely packed fresh flat-leaf parsley leaves

½ cup (25 g) loosely packed fresh mint leaves

¼ cup (25 g) loosely packed fresh oregano

¾ cup (180 ml) fresh lemon juice (from 4 to 6 lemons)

¼ tablespoons (60 ml) red wine vinegar

½ teaspoon crushed red pepper, plus more to taste

Kosher salt, or sub JF Spicy Salt, and freshly cracked black pepper

PROCESS

Drizzle some olive oil in a small skillet over medium heat; when warm, add the garlic and sauté for 20 seconds. Add the cilantro, parsley, mint, oregano, and sautéed garlic to a food processor and pulse until just roughly chopped. Add the lemon juice, red wine vinegar, crushed red pepper, and a pinch of salt and freshly cracked black pepper. Drizzle in the remaining ¼ cup (60 ml) olive oil and pulse for 10 seconds to combine. Let the chimichurri sit in the refrigerator to cool for a few minutes before serving. Store leftovers in an airtight container in the refrigerator for up to 3 days.

GRANDMA LULIE'S ORANGE CRANBERRY SAUCE page 115
MAYO-FREE VEGAN RANCH opposite
SIMPLE TOMATO SAUCE page 118
CREAMY LEMON, GARLIC, AND DILL DRESSING page 115
CHIMICHURRI opposite
SIMPLE MUSTARD VINAIGRETTE page 118

Simple Tomato Sauce

Homemade tomato sauce is so easy to make that I stopped buying it. It's shocking how much sugar and sodium can be found in commercial sauces. This sauce can be used on pasta, chicken Parmesan, spaghetti squash, or really anything you want.

MAKES ABOUT 3½ CUPS (840 ML)

INGREDIENTS

1 can (28 ounces/795 g) whole peeled tomatoes

1 clove garlic, cut in half

1 medium yellow onion (6 ounces/170 g), cut in half

4 tablespoons (55 g) unsalted butter or ghee or vegan butter

¼ teaspoon freshly cracked black pepper

Kosher salt, or sub JF Spicy Salt

PROCESS

In a large saucepan, crush the tomatoes with a large wooden spoon. Add the garlic, onion, butter, freshly cracked black pepper, and salt to taste. Bring to a boil. Reduce the heat and simmer for about 30 minutes. At this point, you can pick out the onion and garlic halves and discard or use an immersion blender to blend it all together for a smoother, more flavorful sauce. Freeze the sauce in an airtight container if not used within 4 days.

Simple Mustard Vinaigrette

Stop buying salad dressing. It's so easy to make and homemade is so much better for you (most store-bought dressings are filled with hidden sugar and seed oils). This is always on rotation in my house—I make it at least five times a week. Make a big batch and store it in the refrigerator for up to a week. Remove 30 minutes prior to using if you notice the oil has hardened.

MAKES ABOUT ¼ CUP (60 ML)

INGREDIENTS

¼ cup (60 ml) olive oil or avocado oil

1 tablespoon red wine vinegar

1 small clove garlic, minced or grated

1 teaspoon Dijon mustard

⅛ teaspoon kosher salt, or sub JF Spicy or JF Universal Salt, plus more to taste

Freshly cracked black pepper

PROCESS

In a small bowl, whisk together the olive oil, red wine vinegar, garlic, and mustard until thoroughly combined. Season with salt and freshly cracked black pepper.

California Guacamole

Growing up in Santa Barbara, California, there was no shortage of avocados (my father always grew them or one of our neighbors did), so guacamole was a staple. I make this constantly in my house as a dip or schmear for a protein or bread. My version has no tomatoes, but feel free to add them at your discretion. **SERVES 2**

INGREDIENTS

2 ripe avocados, pitted and peeled

1 teaspoon fresh lime juice, plus more to finish

1 tablespoon chopped jalapeño chile

2 tablespoons chopped yellow onion

1 tablespoon chopped fresh cilantro

Kosher salt, or sub JF Spicy or JF Universal Salt, and freshly cracked black pepper

PROCESS

In a medium bowl, smash the avocado and lime juice together with the back of a fork until the avocado is chunky. Add half the chopped jalapeño, then taste to determine if you'd like to add more to increase the spice level. Mix in the onion, cilantro, and salt and freshly cracked black pepper to taste. Finish with an extra squeeze of lime on top.

NOTE: *Keep the avocado pits for the bottom of the guacamole bowl to help retain the avocado's color—my mom's trick!*

Simple Enchilada Sauce

Fun fact: Cheese enchiladas are one of my top-five favorite foods. One of my fondest childhood memories from growing up in California is eating them on a perfect saucy plate with a ton of finely chopped white onion, with the rice and pinto beans spilling into each other, creating one dish. It's sauces like these that I wish I had learned to make earlier in life. It's so easy and so much better than those mixes and cans I grew up with. Take the time to make this—trust me, it's worth it. Pro tip: Use the leftover sauce to make killer late-night nachos.
MAKES ABOUT 2½ CUPS (600 ML)

INGREDIENTS

¼ cup (60 ml) avocado oil

2 tablespoons gluten-free flour or self-rising flour

¼ cup (30 g) chili powder

1 can (8 ounces/225 g) tomato sauce

¼ teaspoon ground cumin

¼ teaspoon garlic powder

¼ teaspoon onion powder

½ teaspoon kosher salt, or sub JF Universal Salt, plus more to taste

PROCESS

Heat a medium skillet over medium-high heat. Add the flour and chili powder. Reduce the heat to medium and cook, whisking often to prevent burning, until lightly browned. Gradually whisk the tomato sauce, 1½ cups (360 ml) water, the cumin, garlic powder, onion powder, and salt into the flour and chili powder until a smooth sauce forms. Continue cooking over medium heat for about 10 minutes, until slightly thickened. Season with more salt to taste as needed.

Pico de Gallo

This pico isn't just for tacos—it's truly the most versatile topping. Try this mixed with scrambled eggs, on top of nachos, or combined with leftover rice. I like to make a batch of this and use it over a few days on various recipes. I also find the chopping of these vegetables into perfect tiny bits to be highly therapeutic.

MAKES 3½ TO 4 CUPS (840 TO 960 ML)

INGREDIENTS

- 3 ripe roma tomatoes, seeded and chopped
- 1 medium white onion (6 ounces/ 170 g), finely chopped
- 2 jalapeño chiles, seeded and finely chopped
- 2 tablespoons chopped fresh cilantro, leaves and tender stems
- Kosher salt, or sub JF Universal Salt

PROCESS

In a large bowl, combine the tomatoes, onion, jalapeños, cilantro, and a generous pinch of salt.

Garlicky and Lemony Vegan Whipped Feta Spread

This is funky in the best way and has a really nice tang to it. It's the perfect substitute for vegan cream cheese, with much more flavor. My favorite way to eat it is spread over well-done toast topped with eggs and finely chopped herbs. F cream cheese! This is better. **SERVES 2**

INGREDIENTS

- 4 ounces (115 g) vegan feta cheese (I like Violife brand), crumbled
- 1 clove garlic
- ⅛ teaspoon dried oregano
- ⅛ teaspoon dried parsley
- 1 tablespoon fresh lemon juice
- 2 teaspoons plain almond milk (I like Three Trees), or more as needed
- Kosher salt, or sub JF Spicy Salt

PROCESS

In a blender, pulse together the vegan feta, garlic, oregano, parsley, lemon juice, almond milk, and salt to taste until smooth. Scrape the sides of the food processor to ensure all the ingredients are properly blended. If you want a thinner spread, add more almond milk 1 teaspoon at a time. Taste and adjust the seasoning.

"You'll Never Buy Salsa Again" Salsa

Trust me, this is SO much better than those watery, flavorless "fresh" salsas you find in the refrigerated section at the grocery stores. This batch will last you through multiple taco nights, quick scrambled-egg meals, and post-party nachos. **SERVES 6**

INGREDIENTS

1 can (14½ ounces/415 g) diced San Marzano tomatoes

1 can (14½ ounces/415 g) diced tomatoes with green chiles

3 to 4 cloves garlic

⅔ cup (75 g) chopped white onion

1 to 2 handfuls fresh cilantro leaves

1 teaspoon ground cumin

1 to 2 jalapeño chiles, seeded

1 teaspoon kosher salt, or sub JF Spicy Salt

¼ teaspoon freshly cracked black pepper

¼ teaspoon granulated sugar or coconut sugar

PROCESS

Pulse the tomatoes, tomatoes with green chiles, garlic, onion, cilantro, cumin, jalapeño, salt, freshly cracked black pepper, and sugar in a food processor or blender until you reach your desired salsa consistency. Taste and adjust the salt. Serve immediately or keep in the fridge in an airtight container for up to 4 days.

Mayo-Free Spinach and Artichoke Dip

I'd always been one to go for the spinach and artichoke dip first at parties. That is, until I realized how much mayo and dairy was in it. I was freaked out for years, then decided to create my own. Here is a version without either (if you go for the vegan cream cheese and cheddar) that can be thrown together in minutes before your guests arrive. I literally can eat this entire thing standing up, with potato or tortilla chips and a hit of hot sauce. This one is a great party trick. No one will notice it is not the mayo-laden original. It doesn't taste healthy. And that is a good thing. **SERVES 2 TO 4**

INGREDIENTS

4 ounces (115 g) cream cheese or vegan cream cheese, at room temperature

1 teaspoon Dijon mustard

½ teaspoon kosher salt, or sub JF Spicy Salt

1 teaspoon freshly cracked black pepper

1 jar (12 ounces/400 g) artichoke hearts in extra virgin olive oil with 2 tablespoons reserved brine, chopped

1 bag (10 ounces/280 g) frozen spinach, thawed, squeezed to remove excess liquid, and chopped

4 ounces (115 g) sharp cheddar cheese or plant-based cheese, freshly grated

Tortilla chips, for serving

PROCESS

1 Preheat your broiler to high.

2 In a medium bowl, whisk the cream cheese, mustard, salt, freshly cracked black pepper, and 2 tablespoons of the reserved artichoke brine until combined. Fold in the spinach, artichoke hearts, and cheddar cheese. Transfer to a broiler-proof ramekin and smooth the top. Broil for about 10 minutes, until the cheese is melted and the top is golden brown and bubbly. Serve warm with tortilla chips.

Chip Scoop Salad

Is it salsa? Is it salad? It's whatever you want it to be. This super-clean and easy salad is perfect to scoop up with some grain-free chips or as a bright salad for lunch. This recipe calls for cilantro, but you can throw in any herb of your choice. If you want to add some protein, Mom's Not-Lazy, Lazy Chicken (page 129) and Universal Protein Meatballs (page 78) work really well with this. It's effortless, versatile, and always delicious. You can plan for leftovers, but there won't be any. Trust. Chop everything fine for this for even distribution of ingredients. I also find it highly therapeutic to aim for perfectly dice-size veg. **SERVES 2 TO 4**

INGREDIENTS

1 yellow pepper, finely chopped

1 small red onion (4 ounces/115 g), finely chopped

3 small Persian cucumbers, finely chopped

1 cup (145 g) chopped cherry tomatoes

1 avocado, peeled, pitted, and finely diced

½ cup (75 g) crumbled vegan feta (I like Trader Joe's)

¼ cup (10 g) chopped fresh cilantro

1 tablespoon fresh lime juice

2 tablespoons Simple Mustard Vinaigrette (page 118), plus more to taste

Kosher salt, or sub JF Spicy or JF Universal Salt

Grain-free tortilla chips, for serving

PROCESS

In a large bowl, toss together the yellow pepper, red onion, cucumber, tomatoes, avocado, vegan feta, and cilantro. Drizzle with the lime juice and mustard vinaigrette, season with a generous pinch of salt, and toss again. Taste and add more dressing and seasoning as desired.

DINNER

Clean and Cheesy Pasta Pomodoro

This pasta is dairy-free, gluten-free, grain-free, and insanely delish. The key here is to finish with fresh basil and dairy-free ricotta. It's my favorite PMS meal or when I'm grumpy and want some comfort food. I truly believe this pasta dish has the power to lift your mood. Try it.

SERVES 2 TO 4

INGREDIENTS

1 box (8 ounces/225 g) grain-free spaghetti (I like Jovial)

1 tablespoon olive oil, plus more for drizzling

1 cup (240 ml) Simple Tomato Sauce (page 118)

Freshly cracked black pepper

Kosher salt, or sub JF Spicy Salt

Dairy-free ricotta (I like Kite Hill)

Dairy-free Parmesan, shredded (I like Violife)

Handful fresh basil, thinly sliced

PROCESS

1 Cook the spaghetti in boiling salted water according to the package instructions. Drain, reserving ½ cup (120 ml) pasta water. Rinse the spaghetti lightly to remove the starch residue.

2 In a large skillet, heat the olive oil over medium heat. Add the tomato sauce and reserved pasta water. Cook until the sauce is bubbling and heated thoroughly, about 2 minutes. Turn off the heat, add the cooked pasta, and toss to coat. Taste and season with freshly cracked black pepper and salt. Serve with dairy-free ricotta, shredded dairy-free parm, fresh basil, and a generous drizzle of olive oil.

"Takeout" Cauliflower Fried Rice

When you need some takeout fried rice but want to make sure you are not getting the seed oils or soy in your food, this is an amazing make-at-home version that comes together quickly. Try not to eat the entire portion out of the pan before you plate it. This is my favorite dinner to make for myself when I'm alone or I get home really late. I drench mine in sriracha and go to town. This will be in your weekly rotation of easy, satisfying meals. **SERVES 2 TO 4**

INGREDIENTS

4 tablespoons (60 ml) olive oil (I like Kyoord), plus more as needed

4 large eggs, beaten

Kosher salt, or sub JF Spicy, JF Universal, or JF Curry salt, and freshly cracked black pepper

2 green onions, sliced into ½-inch-thick (12 mm) pieces

1 tablespoon minced fresh ginger

4 cloves garlic, minced

1 bag (24 ounces/680 g) frozen cauliflower rice

1 cup (95 g) shredded green cabbage

½ cup (75 g) petite peas

½ cup (55 g) shredded carrot

1 jalapeño chile, seeded and thinly sliced, plus more for serving

⅓ cup (15 g) chopped fresh cilantro

Sriracha, for drizzling

PROCESS

1 Heat 2 tablespoons of the olive oil in a large skillet or wok over medium-high heat. Add the eggs and cook undisturbed for 20 seconds. Stir to break up the egg into scramble-size pieces and cook for about 1 minute more, until the eggs are cooked through. Season with salt and freshly cracked black pepper. Remove to a plate; set aside.

2 Add the remaining 2 tablespoons oil, the green onions, ginger, and garlic. Cook over medium-high heat, stirring often, until fragrant, about 1 minute. Add the cauliflower rice and more olive oil, if needed. Cook the cauliflower rice for 12 to 15 minutes, stirring at 3- to 5-minute intervals, until crisped and browned. Add the cabbage, peas, carrots, and jalapeños. Toss and cook until the peas are cooked through and the carrots are tender, about 2 minutes. Taste and adjust the seasoning. Turn the heat to low and add the scrambled eggs. Toss to combine.

3 Serve topped with more jalapeños, the cilantro, and a drizzle of sriracha.

The Kids' Favorite Simple Skirt Steak

Pretty much the only cut of steak I make, because it's so flavorful. This is my kids' favorite steak, and the same goes for any of their friends who come over as well. I like to have this marinate in the fridge from A.M. to P.M. and pan-sear fast at night to create easy tacos, rice bowls, and salads for the kids at a moment's notice. Make sure to always cut it against the grain so it's tender. **SERVES 2 TO 4**

INGREDIENTS

1 beef skirt steak (1½ to 2 pounds/ 680 g to 910 g)

1 teaspoon kosher salt, or sub JF Spicy Salt, plus more to taste

½ teaspoon freshly cracked black pepper, plus more to taste

1 teaspoon garlic powder

1 teaspoon onion powder

2 tablespoons olive oil

PROCESS

1 Trim the steak if needed and slice it into 4 to 5 long pieces of steak (it cooks faster, when you're in a rush). In a large bowl, combine the salt, freshly cracked black pepper, garlic powder, and onion powder and mix well. Add the steak pieces to the bowl and toss to coat in the spice blend. Use your hands to evenly distribute and rub the seasoning into the steak. Cover the bowl in plastic wrap and refrigerate for at least 2 hours or overnight.

2 In a large skillet over medium to high heat, heat the olive oil, swirling it to coat the pan. Once the pan is hot, add the pieces of steak and sear them for 2 to 3 minutes on each side. Cook a little longer if you prefer your steak medium to medium-well. Once cooked, let the steaks rest for 5 to 10 minutes before slicing or chopping.

Keto Cheeseburger Bake

This is my version of a burger. Completely keto, but totally hits the spot when there's a hankering for a burger. You can modify this with any toppings of your choice. It's wildly delish smothered in extra melted cheese, ketchup, mustard, onions, and pickles. This is one of those dishes you will be craving at that time of the month or if you're just in need of something comforting and easy to make. It's sort of like a burger quiche in the best way. **SERVES 9**

INGREDIENTS

Ghee or olive oil cooking spray

1 tablespoon olive oil

2 pounds (910 g) ground beef

1 medium yellow onion (6 ounces/170 g), finely chopped

½ teaspoon kosher salt, or sub JF Spicy or JF Universal Salt

½ teaspoon freshly cracked black pepper

6 large eggs

1 cup (240 ml) heavy cream or plain almond milk

1 teaspoon dry mustard

1 teaspoon garlic powder

6 slices American cheese or plant-based American cheese (I like 365 plant-based cheddar style slices; they melt just like American cheese)

For burger toppings

1 head iceberg lettuce, shredded

1 tomato, sliced

1 red onion, sliced

2 dill pickle chips per serving (I like Grillo's)

9 slices bacon, chopped

Mustard

Ketchup

½ cup plus 1 tablespoon (1 tablespoon per serving) Mayo-Free Vegan Ranch (page 116)

PROCESS

1 Preheat the oven to 350°F (175°C). Grease or spray an 8-inch (20 cm) square baking dish with ghee or olive oil cooking spray.

2 Heat the olive oil in a large skillet over medium-high heat. Add the ground beef and onions and sauté, breaking up the meat into small bits, until the beef is browned and the onions are soft, 5 to 7 minutes. Season with the salt and freshly cracked black pepper.

3 In a large mixing bowl, whisk together the eggs, cream or almond milk, dry mustard, and garlic powder. Place the cooked meat in the baking dish, spreading it out so it covers the whole pan. Do not press down. Slowly and evenly pour the egg mixture over the beef. Bake the beef for 20 minutes. Remove from the oven and evenly cover the top of the meat with the cheese slices. Bake for another 8 to 10 minutes, until the cheese is melted. Slice into 9 even square cheeseburgers and serve over shredded iceberg lettuce with your burger toppings and condiments of choice.

Keto Sesame Chicken

I really miss the days when I could indulge in Chinese takeout. But now I've figured out how to make my own at home. I especially love sticky, saucy sesame chicken, and that's what inspired this keto-friendly dish. Serve this with "Takeout" Cauliflower Fried Rice (page 131) for a cleaner alternative to takeout. Kids LOVE this, especially the little ones who use their hands to eat it. My friends swear by this recipe for their toddlers. You'll never want the traditional MSG- and sugar-filled version again. **SERVES 4 TO 6**

INGREDIENTS

For the chicken

3 boneless, skinless chicken breasts (6 to 8 ounces/170 g to 225 g)

2 large eggs

1 cup (130 g) arrowroot flour

2 cups (230 g) blanched almond flour

1 teaspoon kosher salt, or sub JF Spicy Salt

½ teaspoon five-spice powder

½ teaspoon garlic powder

½ teaspoon onion powder

1 cup avocado oil, for frying

For the keto sesame sauce

¼ cup (60 ml) ketchup (I like Good Food For Good)

¼ cup (60 ml) coconut aminos (I like Coconut Secret)

1 tablespoon raw honey

1 tablespoon rice vinegar

1 teaspoon minced garlic

1 teaspoon minced fresh ginger

Crushed red pepper flakes

1 tablespoon toasted sesame oil, plus more to taste

Toasted sesame seeds, for finishing

2 green onions, thinly sliced

PROCESS

Make the chicken

1 Set up your dredging station: In a large bowl, whisk the eggs and arrowroot flour until smooth. In a large plate or baking dish, whisk together the almond flour, salt, five-spice powder, garlic powder, and onion powder. Working in batches, dip the chicken cubes into the egg and arrowroot flour batter, then dredge in the dry ingredients until well coated. Place the batter-fried chicken cubes on a wire rack until ready to fry. Line a plate with paper towels.

2 In a 4-quart (3.8 liter) saucepan over medium-high heat, heat the avocado oil to 350°F (175°C). Fry the coated chicken in batches, tossing frequently, until golden brown, about 8 minutes per batch. Transfer the fried chicken to the paper towel-lined plate.

Make the sesame sauce

3 In a large skillet over medium heat, whisk together the ketchup, coconut aminos, honey, rice vinegar, garlic, ginger, red pepper flakes, and sesame oil. Reduce the heat to low. Cook, whisking constantly, until the sauce has thickened slightly, about 3 minutes.

4 Add the chicken to the sauce and toss to coat thoroughly. Turn off the heat and sprinkle with sesame seeds, the green onions, and more sesame oil, if desired.

Turkey Cauliflower "Stew"

This is a fun take on traditional chili and of course means I get to prep a topping bar for dinner (my favorite thing). I really like to cook this down so it's a stew consistency, which has no residual liquid, so it literally stands on its own. You can also throw this in a casserole dish with cheese for a yummy Sunday bake. Omit the beans if your kids don't dig them. **SERVES 4**

INGREDIENTS

1 pound (455 g) ground turkey

1 teaspoon kosher salt, or sub JF Spicy or JF Universal Salt

½ teaspoon freshly cracked black pepper

1 small yellow onion (4 ounces/115 g), chopped

2 cloves garlic, minced

1 small head cauliflower (1½ pounds/680 g), cut into small florets

2 teaspoon chili powder

1 tablespoon chipotle in adobo sauce, minced

1 teaspoon dried oregano

½ teaspoon crushed red pepper, plus more to taste

¾ teaspoon ground cumin

1 can (14 ounces/400 g) fire-roasted diced tomatoes

1 teaspoon tomato paste

1 can (8 ounces/225 g) tomato sauce

1 cup (240 ml) chicken broth

For the toppings

1 cup (100 to 200 g) shredded Colby Jack cheese or plant-based Colby Jack cheese (I like Violife)

Crushed tortilla chips or grain-free tortilla chips

Sour cream or plain coconut yogurt

1 red onion, thinly sliced

1 or 2 small jalapeño chiles, seeded and thinly sliced

½ cup (10 g) fresh cilantro leaves)

PROCESS

In a large pot over medium-high heat, cook the ground turkey until browned, using a spatula to break it apart into chunks, about 5 minutes. Season with the salt and freshly cracked black pepper. Add the onion and garlic and cook until translucent and the turkey is cooked through. Add the cauliflower, chili powder, chipotle in adobo sauce, oregano, crushed red pepper, and cumin. Mix well, cover, and cook for about 4 minutes, until the cauliflower is tender. Stir in the fire-roasted tomatoes, tomato paste, tomato sauce, and chicken broth. Cover, reduce the heat to low, and cook for about 8 minutes. Uncover and cook for about 12 minutes, until the liquid has reduced slightly. Serve the stew with all the topping ingredients set up as a toppings bar.

Cauliflower Chicken Parm Bake

I love a casserole, so I wanted to try an anti-inflammatory version of one of my favorite deconstructed dishes. The cauliflower rice sub works perfectly here; you won't even miss the pasta. This is perfect for a make-ahead dinner or meal prep. And it even freezes well. Serve this for casual dinner parties or as something to take and bake for a family gathering. It travels well. **SERVES 2**

INGREDIENTS

- 2 tablespoons olive oil
- 1 bag (12 ounces) frozen cauliflower rice
- 1 shallot, chopped
- 1 clove garlic, minced
- 2 tablespoons tomato paste
- 1 tablespoon Korean red pepper flakes (gochujang)
- ½ cup (120 ml) dry white wine
- 4 boneless, skinless chicken breasts (6 to 8 ounces/170 to 225 g), cut into small cubes
- 1 tablespoon onion powder
- 1 tablespoon garlic powder
- ½ teaspoon kosher salt, or sub JF Spicy or JF Universal Salt
- 1 cup (110 g) shredded mozzarella or plant-based mozzarella cheese (I like Violife)
- ½ cup (50 g) shredded Parmesan cheese, or sub plant-based Parmesan (I like Violife brand)
- 2 tablespoons chopped fresh flat-leaf parsley

PROCESS

1. In a medium skillet over medium-high heat, heat 1 tablespoon of the olive oil. Add the cauliflower rice and cook for 12 to 15 minutes, stirring every 3 minutes or so, until browned.

2. Meanwhile, in another medium skillet over medium heat, add the remaining 1 tablespoon olive oil and the shallots. Cook until the shallots are translucent, about 2 minutes. Add the garlic, tomato paste, and red pepper flakes and cook for about 3 minutes, then deglaze with the white wine. Cook until the wine is reduced by half, about 5 minutes. Meanwhile, preheat the broiler to high heat.

3. When the wine is reduced, add the chicken, onion powder, garlic powder, and salt. Stir to combine and cook until the chicken is just cooked through, about 6 minutes. Remove from the heat.

4. In a broiler-safe dish, layer the chicken, cauliflower rice, and shredded cheeses. Broil for about 5 minutes, until the cheese has melted and is lightly browned. Serve topped with the chopped parsley.

Clean Joes

Sloppy Joes are the ultimate messy, delicious comfort food. My version has a slightly sweet tang to it, which makes the melted vegan cheese and pickles a perfect complement. Try this as a sandwich with a bun or on top of nachos or inside a grain-free tortilla as a taco. The possibilities are endless. I've even scrambled leftovers into eggs. Make this for kids with potato buns and they will thank you. **SERVES 4 TO 6**

INGREDIENTS

1 pound (455 g) grass-fed ground beef

½ teaspoon baking soda

1 small yellow onion (4 ounces/115 g), finely chopped

1 red bell pepper (8 ounces/225 g), finely chopped

¾ teaspoon chili powder

½ teaspoon ground cumin

1 teaspoon kosher salt, or sub JF Spicy or JF Universal Salt, plus more to taste

3 cloves garlic, minced

1 tablespoon tomato paste

½ cup (120 ml) ketchup (I like Primal Kitchen)

1 tablespoon chipotle in adobo sauce

1 tablespoon spicy brown mustard (I like Primal Kitchen)

1 tablespoon coconut sugar or maple sugar

½ teaspoon coconut aminos

4 to 6 grain-free hamburger buns, lightly toasted (I like Unbun); alternatively, this can be made into a wrap by using a burrito-size grain-free wrap (I like Coyotas)

4 to 6 slices plant-based cheddar cheese slices (I like 365 Cheddar or Violife)

Pickle slices (about 3 per bun)

PROCESS

1 Put the ground beef and baking soda in a large bowl. Using your hands, break apart and mix the ground beef just until the baking soda is evenly dispersed. Don't overmix. Refrigerate for 15 minutes.

2 Heat a large skillet over medium-high heat. Melt the vegan butter, then add the olive oil; heat for about 45 seconds. When the butter and oil are shimmering and the pan is very hot, add the ground beef and cook, breaking up the beef into large chunks using a rubber spatula. Allow the chunks to brown and crisp, then add the onion and red bell pepper and cook until the onion is translucent and the peppers are tender, about 3 minutes. Season with the chili powder, cumin, and salt. Cook, stirring often, until the spices are evenly coating the beef and vegetables.

3 Add the garlic, tomato paste, ketchup, chipotle in adobo sauce, mustard, coconut sugar, and coconut aminos. Mix to thoroughly combine. Reduce the heat to medium and cook until thickened slightly, about 10 minutes. Taste and adjust the seasoning.

4 Serve the beef filling between toasted grain-free buns with a slice of plant-based cheddar cheese and pickle slices, or as a nacho topping or funky taco.

Ribollita Soup

This is one of my favorite soups to make when I want something that feels really comforting and filling without meat. The original versions are made with stale bread, but you can also double the beans for a gluten-free option that thickens this soup just as well. Feel free to toast a few cubes of toasted grain-free bread with olive oil and throw them in too for a hearty addition. **SERVES 4 TO 6**

INGREDIENTS

2 tablespoons extra-virgin olive oil, plus more to serve

1 large onion (8 ounces/225 g), chopped

2 medium carrots, peeled and chopped

2 stalks celery, chopped

3 cloves garlic, thinly sliced

⅛ teaspoon crushed red pepper

Kosher salt, or sub JF Spicy or JF Universal Salt, and freshly cracked black pepper

1 tablespoon tomato paste

1 bunch Tuscan kale, chopped

1 can (14½ ounces/415 g) diced tomatoes

4 cups (960 ml) low-sodium vegetable or chicken stock

4 to 5 sprigs fresh thyme

1 bay leaf

1 Parmesan rind

1 can (15½ ounces/445 g) cannellini beans, rinsed and drained, plus 1 extra can if omitting the bread

2 cups (240 g) cubed, day-old or stale grain-free or gluten-free bread, toasted (optional)

2 tablespoons grated Parmigiano-Reggiano cheese or plant-based Parmesan (I like Violife)

PROCESS

1 In a large stockpot, heat the olive oil over medium heat. Add the onion, carrots, celery, garlic, and crushed red pepper and cook for 7 to 8 minutes, stirring occasionally, until the vegetables are softened. Season with salt and freshly cracked black pepper. Add the tomato paste and cook for another 1 to 2 minutes. Stir in the kale and cook until it starts to wilt, 3 to 4 minutes. Add the diced tomatoes, stock, thyme, bay leaf, and Parmesan rind and bring to a simmer.

2 Pour about ½ cup (75 g) of the cannellini beans into a small bowl with a couple tablespoons of the cooking liquid and mash them together with a fork to form a paste. Pour the paste into the soup to thicken, then stir in the remaining beans and half of the bread cubes, if using. If not, stir in the extra can of beans. Taste and adjust the seasoning. Cover and simmer over low heat for 15 minutes.

3 Remove the Parmesan rind. Ladle the soup into bowls and top with the grated Parmesan and more toasted bread.

"Float My Boat" Beefy Pesto Zucchini Boats

I'm a HUGE fan of "stuffed" food. Stuffed pasta, peppers, tomatoes—you name it, I'm in. I used to make rice- or dairy-stuffed baked dishes all the time, but not anymore . . . I lean on these zucchini boats to scratch that itch, and, as a bonus, they are filled with the protein we all need more of—not the carbs we don't. **SERVES 4 TO 6**

INGREDIENTS

5 or 6 medium (about 6 ounces/170 g) zucchinis, trimmed on both ends and halved lengthwise

1 teaspoon kosher salt, or sub JF Spicy Salt, plus more for sprinkling

1 tablespoon olive oil

1 clove garlic, minced

1 small yellow onion (4 ounces/115 g), finely chopped

1 pound (455 g) grass-fed ground beef

1 teaspoon freshly cracked black pepper, plus more to taste

1 bag (10 ounces/280 g) frozen cauliflower rice, thawed and squeezed to remove excess water

3 tablespoons vegan pesto, plus more to taste (I like Gotham Greens)

¼ cup (25 g) grated plant-based Parmesan cheese (I like Violife), plus more for serving

Handful chopped fresh flat-leaf parsley, plus more for serving

PROCESS

1 Preheat the oven to 375°F (190°C). Line a large baking sheet with aluminum foil. Using a spoon, scoop the seeds out of the zucchini halves, careful not to make them too thin to stuff. Sprinkle each half with salt. Place on the prepared baking sheet and set aside.

2 Heat the olive oil in a large skillet over medium-high heat. Add the garlic and onion and sauté until translucent, about 2 minutes. Add the beef and season with the salt and freshly cracked black pepper. Using a spatula, break up the beef into large chunks. Allow the chunks to brown before stirring occasionally until the beef is cooked through, about 6 minutes. Drain excess fat if needed. Add the cauliflower rice and the pesto; mix thoroughly. Remove from the heat and add the plant-based Parmesan and a handful of parsley. Taste and adjust the seasoning.

3 Divide the beef and cauliflower filling among the zucchini halves, packing down the filling to fill the bottom of each boat and then slightly overstuffing the tops. Grate extra Parmesan over the top. Bake until the zucchini boats are tender, 30 to 35 minutes. Serve warm topped with more Parmesan, parsley, and a pinch of salt.

"Meatless Monday" Brussels Sprout Tacos

This is one of my favorites for a meatless Monday, because it's not just a salad. It is filling and honestly so delicious. The charred bits of Brussels sprouts add an earthy crunch to each bite. The key (similar to my cauliflower rice technique) is to really leave the Brussels sprouts alone on the hot pan with minimal stirring and let the heat do the trick. Top these tacos with vegan feta, Tia Lupita hot sauce, California Guacamole (page 119), and my good slaw for crunch, all wrapped up in your favorite grain-free tortillas. The leftovers (if any) make a great salad topping served cold for tomorrow's lunch. **SERVES 4 TO 6**

INGREDIENTS

1 tablespoon olive oil, plus more as needed

2 cloves garlic, chopped

1 small yellow onion (4 ounces/115 g), diced

2 poblano chiles, diced

½ teaspoon ground cumin

½ teaspoon ground coriander

1 teaspoon kosher salt, or sub JF Spicy or JF Universal Salt, plus more to taste

2 bags (14 ounces/400 g each) shredded Brussels sprouts

1 jalapeño chile, seeded and diced

6 to 8 grain-free tortillas, toasted (I like Coyotas)

For the toppings

1 recipe JF Slaw (page 105)

1 recipe California Guacamole (page 119)

2 tablespoons crumbled vegan feta cheese (I like Violife)

Hot sauce (I like Tia Lupita), for drizzling

½ cup (15 to 20 g) coarsely chopped fresh cilantro

2 limes, cut into wedges

PROCESS

1 Heat the olive oil in a large skillet over medium-high heat. Once the oil shimmers, add the garlic, onion, and poblanos. Cook until the onions are translucent and the peppers are tender, about 3 minutes. Season with the cumin, coriander, and salt. Add the Brussels sprouts and jalapeño and toss to coat—add more oil if needed. Sauté the Brussels sprouts, stirring occasionally, until charred, 12 to 15 minutes. Taste and adjust the seasoning.

2 Remove from the heat and let cool slightly. Spoon a generous amount of the Brussels sprout filling onto each toasted grain-free tortilla. Top with some slaw, guacamole, vegan feta, hot sauce, cilantro, and a squeeze of fresh lime. Leftover Brussels sprout filling or slaw can be refrigerated in an airtight container in the fridge for up to 2 days.

Taco Soup

Taco soup is the best of both worlds. It is a cross between chili and your favorite hard-shell taco. And it's fast and comforting. I started making this years ago when I wanted something slightly different from my chili recipe. I credit my friend Michelle for first introducing me to a version of this in our cooking club (hers had Fritos). Don't forget to crush your favorite hard taco shells on top, and add as many toppings as you can. The more things you throw on top here the better. This, like most chili- and bean-based soups, tastes better the next day, so if you have time to make ahead and reheat, I recommend it. **SERVES 8**

INGREDIENTS

2 tablespoons avocado oil

1 to 1¼ pounds (455 to 570 g) ground beef

1 medium yellow onion (6 ounces/170 g), chopped

1 cup (145 g) chopped red or yellow bell pepper (about 1 large pepper)

1 large jalapeño chile, seeded and chopped

3 cloves garlic, minced

1½ tablespoons chili powder

1 teaspoon ground cumin

¼ teaspoon dried oregano

¾ teaspoon paprika

1½ teaspoons dried or finely chopped fresh chives

½ teaspoon dried dill

1 teaspoon garlic powder

1 teaspoon onion powder

Crushed red pepper

1 can (15 ounces/430 g) black beans

1 can (15 ounces/430 g) pinto beans

¼ cup (10 g) chopped fresh cilantro

1½ cups (105 g) fresh or frozen corn kernels

Juice of 1 lime (about 2 tablespoons)

2 cans (28 ounce/795 g each) diced tomatoes

1 can (4 ounces/115 g) chopped green chiles

½ teaspoon kosher salt, or sub JF Universal Salt

½ teaspoon freshly cracked black pepper

1¾ cups (420 ml) beef broth

For the toppings

2 cups (220 g) tortilla chips or grain-free chips (I like Siete's salt-free)

1 recipe California Guacamole (page 119)

1 avocado, peeled, pitted, and sliced

½ red onion, chopped

1 recipe Pickled Onions (page 234)

½ cup (120 ml) sour cream or plain coconut yogurt (I like Cocojune)

½ cup (60 g) grated cheddar cheese or plant-based cheese (I like Violife)

1 cup (75 g) chopped iceberg lettuce

½ cup (10 g) chopped fresh cilantro

Pico de Gallo (page 121)

PROCESS

1 Heat the avocado oil in a large saucepan over medium-high heat. Add the ground beef and break up the meat into chunks. Sauté for about 5 minutes, stirring every minute or so, until the meat is browned. Add the onion, bell pepper, jalapeño, and garlic to the pan and sauté for about 4 minutes. Season with the chili powder, cumin, oregano, and paprika; mix to thoroughly combine. Add the chives, dill, garlic powder, onion powder, and crushed red pepper. Mix well and continue to sauté for 2 to 3 minutes.

2 Add the black beans, pinto beans, and cilantro and mix, being careful not to crush the beans too much. Stir in the corn and lime juice. Add the cans of diced tomatoes and green chiles and stir to combine. Season with salt and freshly cracked black pepper. Pour in the beef broth and bring to a boil.

3 Turn the heat to low, cover, and simmer for 15 to 20 minutes. If you can make this the day before and let sit overnight, the flavors will intensify. Serve the soup in individual bowls with a spread of all the toppings.

Basic Late-Night Curry Kelp Noodles

Kelp noodles are the perfect substitute for rice noodles for most dishes. The key is to soften them beforehand, and I'll teach you how below, with help from baking soda and fresh lemon. This curry is always my go-to on busy, cold evenings. So delicious, easy, and completely on the program. The perfect alternative to takeout rice noodles. Trust me, you can't tell the difference. You get the same rice noodle vibe here but with grain-free kelp. **SERVES 4**

INGREDIENTS

2 packages kelp noodles (1 pound/ 455 g each)

2 teaspoons baking soda

Juice of 1 lemon (about 3 tablespoons)

6 cups (1.4 liters) hot water

2 tablespoons olive oil

½ cup (110 g) chopped yellow onion

1 teaspoon minced fresh ginger

2 tablespoons yellow curry paste (I like Mekhala)

1 can (14 ounces/400 g) coconut cream

⅓ cup (15 g) thinly sliced fresh basil leaves, plus more for serving

½ teaspoon kosher salt or sub JF Spicy, JF Universal, or JF Curry salt, plus more to taste

2 cups (190 g) shredded cabbage

½ cup (55 g) shredded carrots

2 tablespoons fresh lime juice, plus lime wedges for serving

½ cup (10 g) chopped fresh cilantro, for serving

PROCESS

1 Drain the kelp noodles and place them in a large bowl. Add the baking soda and lemon juice. Pour the hot water over the noodles and mix well. Let soak for about 10 minutes, until tender, then drain and rinse with cool water. Set aside.

2 Heat the olive oil in a large skillet over medium-high heat. Add the onion and ginger and sauté until fragrant, about 2 minutes. Add the curry paste and cook, stirring often, until the paste is cooked through and begins to darken slightly, about 3 minutes (this step is important because it helps temper the aromatics in the curry). Reduce the heat to medium and add the coconut cream, basil, and salt. Bring to a simmer, then add the noodles, cabbage, and carrots. Toss and cook for about 5 minutes, until the sauce has reduced slightly and the ingredients are evenly coated. Remove from the heat, add the lime juice, and toss again.

3 Taste and season with more salt, if desired. Serve topped with the cilantro, additional basil, and lime wedges.

"Everything That Isn't Chili" Vegan Chili

This is the perfect Sunday comfort dinner and is so great if you're avoiding meat. Enjoy it on its own or throw it into a grain-free tortilla with extra toppings for a riff on a chili burrito. Feel free to also wrap it up in some burrito-size tortillas and broil with cheese on top for a saucy chili and cheese burrito. **SERVES 4 TO 6**

INGREDIENTS

For the cauli-meat

1 large (1½ pounds/680 g) head cauliflower, trimmed and coarsely chopped

1 tablespoon olive oil (I like Kyoord)

1 tablespoon chili powder

1 tablespoon garlic powder

1 tablespoon onion powder

1 teaspoon dried oregano

1 teaspoon smoked paprika, plus more to taste

1½ teaspoons kosher salt, or sub JF Spicy or JF Universal Salt, plus more to taste

For the chili

2 tablespoons olive oil, plus more for drizzling

1 medium yellow onion (6 ounces/170 g), chopped

2 cloves garlic, chopped

1 large carrot (5 ounces/140 g), peeled and chopped

½ cup (70 g) frozen corn kernels

1 large sweet potato (8 ounces/225 g), peeled and cubed

1 bunch Tuscan kale (6 ounces/170 g), trimmed and finely chopped

1 tablespoon concentrated tomato paste

1 teaspoon chopped fresh thyme

½ teaspoon ground cumin

¾ teaspoon ground cinnamon

½ teaspoon smoked paprika

1 tablespoon chili powder

1 can (14½ ounces/415 g) diced fire-roasted tomatoes

4 cups (960 ml) vegetable broth

For the toppings

2 green onions, thinly sliced

½ cup (110 g) shredded vegan cheddar (I like Violife)

1 avocado, sliced

(recipe continues)

PROCESS

Make the cauli-meat

1 Preheat the oven to 450°F (230°C). Line a large baking sheet with aluminum foil. Add the chopped cauliflower to the baking sheet. Drizzle with the olive oil and season with the chili powder, garlic powder, onion powder, oregano, smoked paprika, and salt. Toss to coat. Roast until browned and crisp, about 20 minutes.

Make the chili

2 Heat the olive oil in a large pot or Dutch oven over medium-high heat. Add the onions and garlic; cook until fragrant and the onions are translucent, about 3 minutes. Add the carrots, corn, sweet potato, kale, and tomato paste. Season with the fresh thyme, cumin, cinnamon, smoked paprika, chili powder, and salt; mix well and cook, stirring often, until the spices are toasted, about 2 minutes. Add the tomatoes, vegetable broth, and cauli-meat to the pot. Stir and bring to a boil. Turn the heat to low, cover, and simmer for 15 minutes. Uncover and cook for about 12 minutes more, until the liquid has reduced slightly and the chili has thickened. Taste and adjust the seasoning.

3 Serve in individual bowls topped with green onion, vegan cheddar, and avocado.

Clean Grain-Free Noodle Kugel, Two Ways

I wanted to create a grain-free, dairy-free version of kugel so I could indulge during the Rosh Hashanah holiday festivities. I made both savory and sweet options, which can be baked together or made ahead of time, and they turned out incredible. They are dense and best if eaten warm with gravy, alongside my Simple Slow-Cooker BBQ-Style Brisket (page 224) and "You Won't Miss the Potato" Cauliflower Latkes (page 222). Everyone in your family will be asking you to make these every year now. Sorry. **SERVES 6 TO 8**

INGREDIENTS

For the sweet kugel

½ cup (60 g) raw cashews

¼ cup (60 ml) boiling water

1 tablespoon olive oil

1 tablespoon fresh lemon juice

½ teaspoon kosher salt, or sub JF Spicy Salt, plus more to taste

4 tablespoons unsalted vegan butter (I like Monty's)

2 Fuji apples (4 ounces/115 g each), peeled and chopped

1 teaspoon ground cinnamon

3 tablespoons coconut sugar

¼ cup (60 ml) super-fine blanched almond flour

1 box grain-free spaghetti (8 ounces/225 g), cooked according to package instructions (I like Jovial)

6 large eggs

1 teaspoon pure vanilla extract

For the savory kugel

1 box (8 ounces/225 g) grain-free fusilli, cooked according to package instructions

½ cup (60 g) raw cashews

¼ cup (60 ml) boiling water

1 tablespoon olive oil

1 tablespoon fresh lemon juice

½ teaspoon kosher salt, or sub JF Spicy Salt, plus more to taste

1 clove garlic, peeled

2 tablespoons olive oil

1 small yellow onion (4 ounces/115 g), sliced into long strips

2 tablespoons vegan butter (I like Monty's)

¼ cup (60 ml) super-fine blanched almond flour

6 large eggs

2 tablespoons fried onions, for topping

(recipe continues)

PROCESS

Make the sweet kugel

1 Drain the pasta and set aside. Preheat the oven to 350°F (175°C). Grease an 8-inch (20 cm) square baking pan. Line with parchment paper and grease with nonstick cooking oil spray.

2 In a large bowl, pour the boiling water over the cashews and let sit for 10 minutes. Add the cashews and water to a blender along with the olive oil, lemon juice, salt, and garlic. Blend just until the cashew texture is close to the curd-like texture of cottage cheese. Taste and adjust the seasoning. Set aside.

3 In a medium skillet over medium-high heat, melt 2 tablespoons of the vegan butter. Add the apples and sauté until softened, about 1 minute. Add the cinnamon and 2 tablespoons of the coconut sugar. Sauté until the apples are caramelized, 3 to 5 minutes. Remove from the heat.

4 In a saucepan over medium heat, combine the remaining 2 tablespoons vegan butter, the almond flour, and salt. Cook, stirring constantly, until a crumb-like mixture forms, about 3 minutes.

5 In a large bowl, combine the cooked spaghetti, cashew cream, and half of the apples. In a medium bowl, whisk together the eggs, vanilla, and remaining 1 tablespoon coconut sugar. Pour over the spaghetti and mix well. Pour the spaghetti mixture into a baking dish and top with the almond flour crumbs. Bake for 1 hour and 30 minutes, or until the top is well browned. If desired, place the kugel under a broiler preheated to high for 2 minutes to char the top. Top with the remaining caramelized apples and serve.

Make the savory kugel

1 Drain the pasta and set aside. Preheat the oven to 350°F (175°C)—or leave it on if you just finished making the sweet kugel! Grease an 8-inch (20 cm) square baking pan. Line with parchment paper and grease with nonstick cooking oil spray.

2 In a large bowl, pour the boiling water over the cashews and let sit for 10 minutes. Add the cashews and ¼ cup (60 ml) water to a blender along with the olive oil, lemon juice, and ¼ teaspoon of the salt. Blend until the texture is close to the curd-like texture of cottage cheese. Taste and adjust the seasoning. Set aside.

3 Heat the olive oil in a medium skillet over medium-high heat. Cut the onion in half, removing the outer skin, and slice on its flat side into thin batons. Add the onions and sauté until softened, 3 to 5 minutes. Remove from the heat.

4 In a small saucepan over medium heat, combine the vegan butter, almond flour, and the remaining ¼ teaspoon salt. Cook, stirring constantly, until a crumb-like mixture forms, about 3 minutes.

5 In a large bowl, combine the cooked fusilli, cashew cream, and sautéed onions. In a medium bowl, whisk the eggs and pour over the fusilli. Mix well and transfer into the prepared baking dish. Sprinkle the almond flour crumb mixture over the top and bake for 90 minutes. or until the top of the kugel is well browned. If desired, place the kugel under a broiler preheated to high for 2 minutes to char the top. Top with the fried onions and serve. Once cooled, store in the refrigerator for up to 2 days.

The Best Baked Roasted Pork Tenderloin

This is a recipe that your kids and family will freak out for. It's juicy, herby, and buttery—so perfect cut up in the kids' rice bowls at dinner or on its own with my mashed cauliflower (page 241). It's one of those super simple yet wildly delish proteins that will just make your life easier by giving you a new option for the weekly dinner rotation.

SERVES 4 TO 6

INGREDIENTS

1 pork tenderloin (1½ to 2 pounds/ 680 to 910 g), trimmed

2 tablespoons garlic powder

1 teaspoon dried basil

1 teaspoon dried oregano

1 teaspoon dried thyme

1 teaspoon dried parsley

½ teaspoon dried sage

2 tablespoons olive oil

1 tablespoon kosher salt, or sub JF Spicy or JF Universal Salt

Freshly cracked black pepper

½ cup (1 stick/115 g) butter or vegan butter, sliced into 4 to 6 pats (I like Monty's)

PROCESS

1 Preheat the oven to 350°F (175°C). Line a baking sheet with aluminum foil. In a small bowl, combine the garlic powder, basil, oregano, thyme, parsley, and sage; set aside.

2 Heat a large skillet over medium-high heat. Once the pan is hot, add the olive oil and heat until it shimmers. Season the pork tenderloin with the salt on all sides. Transfer the pork to the pan and sear for 2 to 3 minutes per side, until well browned on all sides.

3 Transfer the pork to the foil-lined baking sheet. Sprinkle with the herb mixture and coat well on all sides. Place the pats of butter on the top of the pork. Wrap the pork tightly in foil and bake for about 25 minutes, until the meat registers 150°F (65°C) on an instant-read thermometer at the widest, thickest part of the tenderloin.

4 Remove the pork from the oven and let it rest, tented in foil, for at least 5 minutes. Transfer the roast to a cutting board. Slice the meat against the grain and serve immediately.

5 Store leftovers in an airtight container in the refrigerator for up to 3 days. Or to freeze leftovers, place the sliced pork in a plastic bag or wrap in plastic wrap and keep in the freezer for up to 3 weeks. To reheat, let the pork thaw naturally in the refrigerator overnight, then remove the plastic and wrap in foil. Bake in an oven preheated to 350°F (175°C) until piping hot, about 15 minutes.

"So Simple It's Silly" Oven-Baked Chicken Thighs

Trust me, this is the easiest protein to pull together in less than 40 minutes. This dinner is always a huge hit in my house. The key is to season the chicken thighs well and let them absorb the spices overnight. If you have no time to marinate them, don't sweat; they will be amazing anyway. The key is rubbing extra olive oil on the skin so it gets nice and crispy. **SERVES 4**

INGREDIENTS

- 1 teaspoon paprika
- 1 teaspoon dried oregano
- 1 teaspoon dried thyme
- 1 teaspoon garlic powder
- 1 teaspoon onion powder
- 1½ teaspoons kosher salt, or sub JF Spicy Salt
- 1 teaspoon freshly cracked black pepper
- 8 to 10 boneless, skinless chicken thighs
- Olive oil, for drizzling

PROCESS

1. In a small bowl, mix the paprika, oregano, thyme, garlic powder, onion powder, salt, and pepper.
2. Place the chicken thighs on a foil-lined baking sheet. Sprinkle the spice blend over the chicken thighs and rub the spices in using your hands.
3. If possible, allow the thighs to marinate in the refrigerator for at least for 6 hours or ideally overnight.
4. Remove the chicken from the refrigerator 30 minutes before baking. Preheat the oven to 400°F (205°C). Add a generous drizzle of olive oil to the chicken thighs and rub it in using your hands. Bake for 22 to 25 minutes, until the thighs are a deep golden brown and an instant-read thermometer inserted into the thickest part of the thigh registers 165°F (75°C).

"Don't Be Afraid of Clams" Vongole Pasta

This is the easiest pasta to throw together if you can find fresh small littleneck clams. The smaller the better and most tender in my opinion. Perfect for a casual group dinner and a great way to get your kids to start eating clams. This is how I enticed Drew to start eating them. The sauce is so delicious; just try not to drink it. **SERVES 2 TO 4**

INGREDIENTS

2 dozen littleneck clams

1 box (8 ounces/225 g) grain-free linguine of your choice or Jovial grain-free spaghetti

6 tablespoons (90 ml) olive oil

5 cloves garlic, minced

½ teaspoon crushed red pepper, plus more for serving

½ cup (70 g) minced shallot

¼ cup (13 g) chopped flat-leaf parsley, plus more for serving

½ cup (120 ml) white wine

1 teaspoon lemon zest

1 tablespoon fresh lemon juice, plus more for serving

3 tablespoons salted butter or vegan butter (I like Monty's or Violife)

Kosher salt, or sub JF Spicy Salt

PROCESS

1 About 20 minutes before starting to cook, put the clams in a large bowl and cover with cold water to expel any sand that might be trapped in them. Run each clam individually under water and then place them in a colander set over a bowl to catch any dripping. Refrigerate until ready to use.

2 Bring a large pot of generously salted water to a boil over medium-high heat. Add the pasta and cook according to the package directions. Reserve ⅓ cup (70 ml) pasta water, then drain the pasta in a colander.

3 Rinse the large pot and return it to medium-high heat on the stovetop. Heat the olive oil, garlic, and crushed red pepper. Add the shallots and cook until translucent, about 1 minute. Add the parsley, white wine, and reserved pasta water. Cook for about 3 minutes, until the liquid is slightly reduced. Stir in the clams. Cover and cook for 6 to 8 minutes, until the clams open up. Uncover the pot and discard any clams that are still closed.

4 Reduce the heat to low and stir in the lemon zest and juice. Add the butter and swirl the pan to melt. Transfer the cooked pasta to the pot and toss to coat in the sauce. Taste and adjust the seasonings. Serve the pasta topped with more crushed red pepper, lemon juice, and parsley.

Mom's Not Lazy, Lazy Chicken

Those who know me know I make this chicken on repeat. It's fast, easy, and inexpensive. Perfect for the nights you have no time (like every night for me) or need a fast-to-meal-prep protein. I promise your entire family will love it. This will be your new in-a-hurry chicken recipe. **SERVES 4**

INGREDIENTS

2 boneless, skinless chicken breasts (6 to 8 ounces/170 to 225 g each)

½ teaspoon kosher salt, or sub JF Spicy, JF Universal, or JF Curry salt

Freshly cracked black pepper

1 teaspoon garlic powder

1 teaspoon onion powder

2 tablespoons Simple Mustard Vinaigrette (page 118)

2 tablespoons olive oil

PROCESS

1 Slice the chicken breasts through the middle into 4 thinner halves.

2 In a large bowl, combine the chicken breasts, salt, freshly cracked black pepper to taste, the garlic powder, onion powder, and mustard vinaigrette. Toss using tongs until the chicken is evenly coated. If you have time to do this in advance, let marinate for at least an hour or overnight, but you can also cook the chicken immediately.

3 Heat the olive oil in a large nonstick pan over medium-high heat. Add the chicken breasts and cook until golden brown, about 5 minutes. Flip and cook until the chicken breasts are cooked all the way through, about 5 minutes. Remove the chicken to a plate and allow to rest for 5 minutes. Cut crosswise into slices or small cubes. Refrigerate in an airtight container in the fridge to use for school lunches or school-night dinners all week long.

Feta and Spinach Chicken Meatballs with Lemony Cauliflower Mash

This is one of my favorite recipes when I need something comforting and want to feel my fork drag through some mash with a yummy meatball. It's on my top-five list for best weeknight dinners. You won't miss the potatoes here, trust me; this cauliflower mash is much lighter than traditional mashed potatoes. **MAKES 12 TO 18 MEATBALLS**

INGREDIENTS

For the chicken meatballs

1 pound (455 g) ground chicken

½ cup (75 g) crumbled vegan feta (I like Violife)

2 cups (60 g) finely chopped spinach or frozen thawed spinach (be sure to dry the fresh spinach well or squeeze out excess moisture from the thawed spinach)

3 cloves garlic, minced

1 small yellow onion (4 ounces/115 g), finely chopped

1½ teaspoons kosher salt, or sub JF Spicy or JF Universal Salt, plus more to taste

2 tablespoons chopped fresh flat-leaf parsley, plus more for serving

½ teaspoon dried oregano

¼ teaspoon dried thyme

¼ teaspoon crushed red pepper

2 tablespoons olive oil (I like Kyoord), plus more for drizzling

½ teaspoon freshly ground black pepper

For the cauliflower mash

⅔ cup (165 ml) low-sodium chicken broth

Kosher salt, or sub JF Spicy or JF Universal Salt

1 small head cauliflower (1½ pounds/680 g), cut into florets

2 tablespoons cream cheese or vegan cream cheese (I like Violife)

1 tablespoon olive oil, plus more for serving

2 tablespoons fresh lemon juice

½ teaspoon garlic powder

1 tablespoon unsalted butter or vegan butter, chilled

Freshly grated Parmesan or vegan Parmesan (I like Violife; optional)

(recipe continues)

PROCESS

Make the chicken meatballs

1 Preheat the oven to 400°F (205°C). Line a large baking sheet with aluminum foil. In a large bowl, combine the chicken, feta, spinach, garlic, onion, salt, parsley, oregano, thyme, crushed red pepper, and olive oil. Work the ground chicken mixture together with your hands (I like to use disposable kitchen gloves) or a metal spoon until just combined, taking care not to overmix.

2 Using your hands, form 12 to 18 uniform meatballs and place on the prepared baking sheet with space between them. Bake for about 12 minutes, until the meatballs are golden brown with an internal temperature of 165°F (75°C) and the juices run clear.

Make the cauliflower mash

3 While the meatballs are baking, warm the chicken broth in a small saucepan over medium heat. Bring a large pot of salted water to a boil. Add the cauliflower florets and boil until fork tender, about 8 minutes. Transfer the cauliflower to a blender along with the warm chicken broth, cream cheese, olive oil, lemon juice, garlic powder and salt to taste. Blend until smooth. Taste and adjust the seasoning. Add the chilled butter and blend the cauliflower mixture for 10 seconds, or until creamy.

Assemble the dish

4 Spread the cauliflower mash on a large plate. Top with the meatballs. Finish with parsley, a drizzle of olive oil, a sprinkle of salt, and Parmesan, if using.

Salt and Pepper Ribs and Wings

My father was known to make his famous ribs and wings on the grill for every family gathering. I've modified his grill technique to make these "city-style," aka in the broiler instead of an outdoor grill. The star here is the special spice blend I've replicated in my father's memory. It's simple and spot-on (sorry, Pops, it has less salt than yours, but I think you would still approve). And yes, you can also throw these on the outdoor grill to make the original version. These will become the "meat on a stick" staple in your house in the weekly family menu rotation, just because they are that freakin' good. Ribs are a great protein—you can feel good about eating them here, because they are free of the usual cane sugar–filled sauces.

SERVES 6 TO 8

INGREDIENTS

For the salt and pepper spice blend

2 teaspoons kosher salt, or sub JF Spicy or JF Universal Salt

1 teaspoon freshly cracked black pepper

2 tablespoons garlic powder

2 tablespoons onion powder

1 teaspoon sweet or smoked paprika

For the ribs

2 racks pork baby back ribs, ideally pasture-raised

For the wings

4 pounds (1.8 kg) chicken wings

Olive oil, for drizzling

PROCESS

Make the spice rub

1 In a small bowl, mix together the salt, freshly cracked black pepper, garlic powder, onion powder, and paprika.

If making ribs

2 If the ribs include the back membrane, trim them to remove. With extreme caution, slide your finger or a knife under the rubbery back membrane. Once you loosen a section, pull it up and off. Slice the ribs into singles.

3 Put the ribs in a large bowl and sprinkle with the spice blend. Toss until the ribs are evenly coated. Refrigerate for at least 6 hours or up to 24 hours.

(recipe continues)

4 Remove the ribs from the refrigerator 30 minutes prior to cooking and bring to room temperature. Preheat the broiler to 500°F (260°C) or high. Place the ribs on a broiler rack with a drip tray (alternatively, you can cook the ribs on wire racks set above two large aluminum foil-lined baking sheets). Broil for 10 minutes, then flip and broil for another 10 minutes. The ribs are done when dark brown and slightly charred. Serve immediately.

If making wings

5 Put the wings in a large bowl and sprinkle with the spice blend. Toss to coat evenly. Place the wings skin side up on a broiler rack with a drip tray or on wire racks set over two large aluminum foil-lined baking sheets. Allow an inch or two (2.5 to 5 cm) in between each wing (crowding the wings will make them steam, which will prevent crispy skin). Refrigerate for at least 3 hours or overnight.

6 Remove the wings from the refrigerator 30 minutes prior to cooking and bring to room temperature. Move the oven rack to the upper-third of the oven. You want enough space to be able to cook the wings without burning them. Preheat the broiler to 500°F (260°C) or high. Drizzle the wings with olive oil and broil for 10 minutes, or until the skin has crisped. Flip and broil for another 8 to 10 minutes, until browned and crispy and the internal temperature reaches 160°F (70°C) on an instant-read thermometer. Serve immediately.

Kevin's Broccoli Soup

This is one of my earlier recipes that I made public. I made this one night when Kevin was under the weather, and we've never looked back. He loves this soup so much he wants us to package and sell it. It's the perfect reason to bust out your immersion blender and make something so simple that the entire family will love it. Top it with herbs, bacon, or your favorite grated cheese. I offer vegan and grain-free options for the ingredients too. It's a great side for the Veginator sandwich (page 86) for a cozy lunch or casual dinner. **SERVES 4 TO 6**

INGREDIENTS

1 tablespoon salted butter, ghee, or vegan butter

1 tablespoon olive oil

3 cloves garlic, minced

1 large yellow onion (8 ounces/225 g), coarsely chopped

1 large carrot, peeled and chopped

1 pound (455 g) broccoli, cut into coarse florets with 2-inch (5 cm) stalks

2 tablespoons all-purpose flour or blanched almond flour

½ cup (120 ml) light cream or almond milk

4 cups (960 ml) low-sodium chicken broth or vegetable broth

Kosher salt, or sub JF Spicy or JF Universal Salt, and freshly cracked black pepper

PROCESS

1 In a stockpot, melt the butter with the olive oil over medium heat. Add the garlic and onion and cook for 2 minutes, or until the onion is translucent. Add the carrot and broccoli. Cook for another 5 minutes, or until the onions start to brown slightly. Add the flour and cook for 1 minute. Add the cream and broth and stir to combine. Bring to a boil, then turn down the heat to low. Cover the pot and simmer for 15 minutes, or until the broccoli is fork tender.

2 Remove the pot from the heat. Using an immersion blender, blend the soup until all the vegetables are pureed and the soup is smooth with a bit of texture. Season with salt and freshly cracked black pepper to taste. Store leftover soup in an airtight container in the fridge for up to 3 days.

Sesame-Crusted Cod with Spicy Slaw

I'm not a fishy fish gal, so I stick to white fish for most of my recipes. Cod was one of the first fish I cooked when I used to make my kids fish sticks during their baby years. To me, these are an "adult" version of fish sticks with a crust made with black and white sesame seeds. I serve mine over a spicy slaw with hot sauce and pickled ginger on the side. Don't skimp on the slaw here—it makes the dish. **SERVES 2 TO 4**

INGREDIENTS

For the spicy slaw

1 cup (70 g) sliced red cabbage

1 cup (70 g) sliced green cabbage

¼ cup (30 g) sliced red onion

1 tablespoon seeded and thinly sliced jalapeño chile

¼ cup (10 g) chopped fresh cilantro

¼ cup (60 ml) Simple Mustard Vinaigrette (page 118)

Kosher salt, or sub JF Spicy Salt

For the fish

2 wild-caught skinless cod fillets (6 ounces/170 g each)

½ teaspoon kosher salt, or sub JF Spicy or JF Universal Salt, plus more for seasoning the fish

Freshly cracked black pepper

2 tablespoons black sesame seeds

2 tablespoons white sesame seeds

½ teaspoon ground cumin

½ teaspoon smoked paprika

½ teaspoon onion powder

Olive oil, for drizzling

For serving

½ cup (10 g) coarsely chopped fresh cilantro

Hot sauce (I like Siete Jalapeño Botano), for drizzling

¼ cup (35 g) pickled jalapeño chiles

2 limes, cut into wedges

2 nori sheets (I like Gimme's Avocado or Olive Oil sheets)

(recipe continues)

PROCESS

Make the spicy slaw

1 In a large bowl, combine the green and red cabbage, red onion, jalapeño, and cilantro. Toss with the mustard vinaigrette, season to taste with salt, and set aside.

Make the fish

2 Preheat the oven to 425°F (220°C). Line a baking sheet with aluminum foil and set aside. Season the cod fillets with a generous sprinkle of salt and set them on a paper towel-lined plate. Chill for 20 minutes—they will leech some water. Remove the fish from the fridge and dry well with a paper towel.

3 Put the black and white sesame seeds in a shallow dish and set aside. In a large bowl, combine the cumin, smoked paprika, onion powder, and ½ teaspoon salt. Using tongs or your hands, dip the cod fillets into the spice blend and turn to coat the fish, making sure that all sides are evenly coated. Drizzle the fillets with olive oil, then transfer to a shallow pan with the sesame seeds and turn to coat until all sides are evenly coated with sesame seeds.

4 Put the fillets on the prepared baking sheet and drizzle with additional olive oil. Bake for 10 to 12 minutes, until the fillets are translucent and cooked through. Let the fish rest on the pan for 2 minutes.

5 Serve the fillets with the slaw. Top with cilantro, hot sauce, and pickled jalapeños with a squeeze of fresh lime, wrapped in some nori.

Crunchy Korean Beef Wraps

There is nothing better than a build-your-own wrap situation. I especially love lettuce wraps, because they are so customizable. You can switch up the beef in this recipe with pretty much any other ground meat. If you want a lighter option, sub in ground turkey or chicken—they are just as yummy. Plus there is something so satisfying about a sweet sesame sauce that is totally free of refined sugars and seed oil. Set this one up as a build-your-own-wrap bar for family and friends for a fun interactive dinner. **SERVES 6 TO 8**

INGREDIENTS

For the sesame sauce

¼ cup (35 g) packed maple sugar (I like Crown Maple) or packed light brown sugar

½ teaspoon crushed red pepper

½ cup (120 ml) coconut aminos

1 teaspoon minced fresh ginger

4 teaspoons toasted sesame oil

For the beef filling

2 pounds (910 g) grass-fed 80/20% ground beef

1 teaspoon baking soda

2 tablespoons olive oil

4 cloves garlic, minced

1 teaspoon minced fresh ginger

½ teaspoon kosher salt or sub JF Spicy Salt

For serving

8 to 10 romaine leaves, washed and dried (iceberg works well too)

Sriracha sauce, or hot sauce of your choice

Vegan kimchi (I like Goshen)

2 green onions, sliced on the diagonal

Chili oil, for drizzling

Toasted sesame oil, for drizzling

White and black sesame seeds, or a combination

JF Spicy Salt

(recipe continues)

PROCESS

Prepare the sesame sauce

1 In a small bowl, combine the maple sugar, crushed red pepper, coconut aminos, ginger, and sesame oil; whisk to combine.

Make the beef filling

2 In a large bowl, combine the ground beef and baking soda. Using your hands, break apart the ground beef and mix just until the baking soda is evenly dispersed. Don't over mix. Refrigerate for 15 minutes. (The baking soda helps crisp up the beef!)

3 In a large skillet over medium-high heat, heat the olive oil for about 45 seconds, until the pan is very hot (a hot pan ensures proper browning and helps prevent the ground beef from leeching too much moisture during the cooking process). Remove the beef from the refrigerator and add to the pan with the garlic, ginger, and salt. Cook, breaking up the beef into large chunks using a rubber spatula, until the chunks are browned before stirring and breaking up the pieces again. (If the beef releases a ton of liquid, drain into a heat-safe bowl and discard once cool.)

4 Reduce the heat to medium. Add the sesame sauce to the beef and mix to combine. Cook, stirring occasionally, until the sauce has reduced and thickened, 8 to 10 minutes. Taste and adjust the seasoning.

5 Set up a build-your-own-wrap bar with the beef filling, lettuce leaves for wrapping, and all the toppings so everyone can serve themselves.

Grain-Free Feta Lasagne

By now you can tell that most of my recipes are either fresh and crisp or comforting and warm. This one falls in the latter category and is effortless and versatile. Any ground meat can be swapped as the protein (it's delicious with ground chicken). I normally use hearts of palm lasagne for this recipe, but you can substitute thinly sliced (#2 on a mandoline) zucchini or eggplant (or both) for a fresher, more veggie-forward dish. Just be sure to salt the slices of zucchini and eggplant and pat them dry to get rid of the extra moisture before using. **SERVES 2 TO 4**

INGREDIENTS

7 ounces (200 g) feta or vegan feta cheese (I like Violife), crumbled

⅔ cup (65 g) shredded Parmesan or vegan Parmesan (I like Violife)

1 package (12 ounces/340 g) Palmini hearts of palm lasagne (or thinly sliced eggplant or zucchini, salted and patted dry)

1 tablespoon olive oil

2 stalks celery, finely chopped

1 medium carrot, peeled and finely chopped

2 cloves garlic, minced

1 small yellow onion (4 ounces/115 g), finely chopped

1 shallot, finely chopped

1 teaspoon dried oregano

1 teaspoon dried thyme

¾ teaspoon kosher salt, or sub JF Spicy Salt, plus more to taste

Crushed red pepper

1 pound (455 g) grass-fed beef

1 can (14 ounces/400 g) cherry tomatoes

PROCESS

1 Preheat the oven to 350°F (175°C). In a medium bowl, combine the vegan feta and Parmesan; set aside. Fill a shallow pot with water and bring to a boil. Add the pieces of hearts of palm lasagne and let sit and soften for 5 to 10 minutes. Remove the soaked lasagne pieces to a paper towel-lined plate and pat dry. Set aside.

2 Heat the olive oil in a large skillet over medium-high heat. Sauté the celery and carrots in the oil until the vegetables are tender, 6 to 8 minutes. Add the garlic, onion, shallot, oregano, thyme, salt, and crushed red pepper to taste. Sauté until the onions are translucent, about 5 minutes. Add the ground beef and cook, stirring often until the meat is almost completely browned, about 3 minutes. Stir in the cherry tomatoes, breaking up the tomatoes with the spatula. Stir and cook until the sauce comes to a boil. Reduce the heat to low and simmer, stirring often to prevent sticking, until the sauce has reduced and thickened, about 8 minutes. Remove from the heat.

3 In the bottom of a 4½ by 8½-inch (11 by 21.5 cm) loaf pan, add a layer of beef and tomato sauce. Top with a layer of the feta and Parmesan mixture, then a layer of the Palmini lasagne positioned horizontally to cover the length of the pan. Spread thicker layers of beef and tomato sauce on top of the lasagne and repeat the layering process until you've used up all the lasagne pieces. Top the final layer with the rest of the cheese mixture.

4 Bake the lasagne for about 25 minutes, until the top starts to bubble and brown. Let sit for 8 minutes to allow the lasagne to cool slightly and firm up before slicing and serving. Once cooled, store in the refrigerator for up to 2 days. Slice and reheat in the oven at 350°F (175°C), or in the microwave, until heated through.

Deconstructed Stuffed Pepper Soup

I love creating "deconstructed" soups based on my favorite dishes. If you love stuffed peppers, this is the soup for you. I also love to top leftovers of this soup with vegan cheddar and scoop it up with tortilla chips. **SERVES 6 TO 8**

INGREDIENTS

2 tablespoons olive oil

I small yellow onion (4 ounces/115 g), finely diced

2 cloves garlic, minced

2 pounds (910 g) grass-fed ground beef (preferably 90/10%)

1 jalapeño chile, seeded and chopped

2 green bell peppers, seeded and chopped

1 red bell pepper, seeded and chopped

1½ teaspoons kosher salt, or sub JF Spicy Salt or JF Universal Salt

1 teaspoon paprika

1 teaspoon freshly cracked black pepper

1 can (16 ounces/480 ml) tomato sauce

1 can (28 ounces/840 ml) diced tomatoes

2 teaspoons beef bouillon

3½ cups (720 g) cooked white rice or cauliflower rice

For the toppings:

Fresh flat-leaf parsley, chopped

Green onion, sliced

Parmesan cheese or vegan Parmesan, shaved (I like Violife)

PROCESS

1 Heat the olive oil in a large stockpot or Dutch oven over medium-high heat. Add the onion, garlic, and ground beef and sauté, stirring often, until the beef is browned, about 5 minutes. Add the jalapeño and green and red bell peppers. Season with the salt, paprika, and freshly cracked pepper. Cook, stirring often, until the peppers are tender, about 3 minutes. Add the tomato sauce, diced tomatoes, beef bouillon, and 6 cups (1.4 liters) water; stir to combine. Bring to a boil, then reduce the heat to low. Cover and simmer for 30 minutes. Uncover, add the cooked rice, and simmer for 10 minutes more. Taste and adjust the seasoning.

2 Serve the soup in individual bowls topped with parsley, sliced green onions, and Parmesan.

Faux Fried-Cauliflower Cutlet

This faux fried-cauliflower cutlet is very similar to a schnitzel (the key is to thinly slice the cauliflower so it cooks through easily). This cutlet is grain-free, gluten-free, and baked, not fried. It has that perfect crispy bite thanks to a fresh, crunchy slaw. But feel free to personalize it with your favorite toppings and sauces. Serve it without a bun and with a grainy mustard and a lemon wedge for a true vegan schnitzel vibe. **SERVES 4 TO 6**

INGREDIENTS

For the slaw

2 cups (195 g) shredded cabbage

¼ cup (30 g) sliced red onion

½ cup (55 g) shredded carrot

½ jalapeño chile, seeded and thinly sliced

2 teaspoons rice wine vinegar

1 tablespoon olive oil

1 tablespoon fresh lemon juice

¼ teaspoon kosher salt, or sub JF Spicy or JF Universal Salt, plus more to taste

⅛ teaspoon coconut sugar

For the cauliflower cutlets

1 small head cauliflower (1½ pounds/680 g)

½ teaspoon kosher salt, plus more for salting the cooking water

2 large eggs

2 tablespoons unsweetened almond milk

2 cups (230 g) blanched almond flour

1 teaspoon smoked paprika

½ teaspoon garlic powder

½ teaspoon onion powder

10 grinds freshly cracked black pepper

4 to 6 grain-free hamburger buns, sliced and toasted (I like Unbun)

2 tablespoons Mayo-Free Vegan Ranch (page 116)

Pickle spears (I like Grillo's Hot Pickles)

PROCESS

Make the slaw

1 In a large bowl, toss together the cabbage, red onion, carrots, and jalapeños. Dress in the rice wine vinegar, olive oil, and lemon juice. Season with the salt and coconut sugar. Set aside.

Make the cauliflower cutlets

2 Trim and discard the leaves from the cauliflower. Remove the bottom core (do not remove the internal core, as that helps the florets stay together). Quarter the cauliflower through the core, then cut each quarter into ¼-inch-thick (6 mm) slices. Reserve any loose cauliflower florets for another use.

3 Preheat the oven to 425°F (220°C). Line a large baking sheet with aluminum foil, then place a wire rack on top. Spray the wire rack with avocado oil spray. In a large, shallow 3-quart (2.8 liter) pan (such as a high-sided skillet or rondeau), heat 2 inches (5 cm) generously salted water to boiling. Add the cauliflower cutlet pieces and blanch until crisp tender, 6 to 8 minutes. Carefully transfer the cauliflower to a paper towel–lined plate, then onto a wire rack to release steam.

4 In a large bowl, whisk the eggs and almond milk. In a shallow medium baking pan, whisk together the almond flour, smoked paprika, garlic powder, onion powder, salt, and freshly cracked black pepper. Coat the cauliflower cutlets in the egg wash, then dredge them in the almond flour breading until evenly coated. The cutlets are fragile, so be gentle during this step.

5 Grease one side of each slice of breaded cauliflower with avocado oil spray. Place the cauliflower, oiled side down, on the prepared rack and roast for about 20 minutes, until golden brown. Remove the cauliflower from the oven and spray the top with avocado oil spray. Flip and bake for 15 minutes more, or until crisp and golden brown. Use a fork to "poke" a cauliflower cutlet to make sure it's tender before removing the cutlets from the oven.

6 Spread one side of the toasted buns with mayo-free ranch. Top each bun with a cauliflower cutlet and about ¼ cup (35 g) slaw, then close the buns and serve.

GATHERINGS, HOLIDAYS & PARTIES

Pad Thai Nachos

Nachos are one of my top-five favorite foods, and pad Thai isn't too far off. This dish is the perfect marriage of both. It's great for a casual appetizer or when you're in the mood for a simple sheet pan dinner that isn't just roasted vegetables and protein. Or serve this on game day for a fun alternative to traditional nachos. Feel free to sub in chopped almonds for finishing instead of peanuts if you have an allergy—or skip the nuts altogether. **SERVES 4 TO 6**

INGREDIENTS

½ cup (120 ml) smooth unsweetened almond butter (I like Base Culture)

3 tablespoons Thai chili paste

⅓ cup (120 ml) tamarind paste (if you can't find this, you are fine to skip it)

1 tablespoon coconut sugar

2 tablespoons coconut aminos

3 cloves garlic, minced

¼ teaspoon kosher salt, or sub JF Spicy Salt

1 boneless, skinless chicken breast (6 to 8 ounces/170 to 225 g), cut into cubes

½ bag (2½ ounces/70 g) grain-free tortilla chips (I like Siete's salt-free)

1 cup (115 g) shredded sharp cheddar or plant-based cheddar cheese (I like Violife)

1 tablespoon olive oil or avocado oil

1 cup (110 g) shredded carrots

3 green onions, roughly chopped into thick pieces on the diagonal

2 cups (180 g) bean sprouts

For serving

1 tablespoon sesame oil

Juice of 1 to 2 limes (about 2 tablespoons)

½ cup (75 g) pickled jalapeño chiles

2 tablespoons crushed peanuts or almonds (optional)

Sriracha, for drizzling (optional)

PROCESS

1 In a large bowl, whisk the almond butter, Thai chili paste, tamarind paste (if using), coconut sugar, coconut aminos, garlic, and salt to form a thick marinade. Add the diced chicken and mix well to coat the chicken. Refrigerate for 20 minutes.

2 Line a large baking sheet with aluminum foil. Spread the grain-free chips on the baking sheet, then evenly sprinkle half the cheddar over the top. Set aside.

3 Heat the olive oil in a large skillet over medium heat. Add the chicken (be sure to scrape all the marinade into the pan as well—this will turn into your sauce) and cook, turning often, until the exterior of the chicken is browned, about 5 minutes. Add 2 tablespoons water, then the carrots and green onions. Cook for about 1 minute, mixing often, until the vegetables soften slightly and the sauce coats all the ingredients. Remove from the heat and preheat the broiler on high.

4 Evenly layer the chicken and the vegetables over the chips. Using tongs, mix up the ingredients just enough so some of the chicken and the sauce get to the chips at the bottom of the baking sheet. Sprinkle the bean sprouts and the remaining cheese over the top and broil for about 5 minutes, until the cheese has melted. Serve the nachos with a drizzle of sesame oil and lime juice. Top with the pickled jalapeños and peanuts and sriracha, if using.

Brunch Enchiladas with Homemade Sauce

Eggs and enchiladas are a dream meal, in my opinion. Make these for your next brunch or for a family holiday breakfast. I like to think that this is the perfect hangover meal, too. People will freak out when they try these enchiladas, as they are not only wildly delish with lots of fun toppings but impressive-looking, too. Also, the enchilada sauce is so easy to make you'll never buy it in cans again. **SERVES 8 TO 10**

INGREDIENTS

18 large eggs

1 tablespoon avocado oil

6 green onions, thinly sliced

2 tablespoons chopped fresh cilantro

2 jalapeño chiles, seeded and finely diced

2 ripe medium tomatoes (4 ounces/115 g each), seeded and finely diced

1 recipe Simple Enchilada Sauce (page 119)

12 small corn or cassava tortillas

2 cups (230 g) grated Colby Jack cheese or plant-based Mexican-blend cheese (I like Violife)

For serving

1 recipe California Guacamole (page 119)

1 recipe Pico de Gallo (page 121)

1 cup (240 ml) plain coconut yogurt (I like Cocojune brand)

PROCESS

1. Preheat the oven to 350°F (175°C).

2. In a large bowl, whisk the eggs thoroughly; set aside. Heat the avocado oil in a large skillet over medium heat. Add the green onions and jalapeño and sauté until softened, about 3 minutes. Pour the whisked eggs into the skillet and turn the heat to medium-low. Let cook without stirring until the edges of the eggs are just barely set but the center is still raw. Using a rubber spatula, gently swipe across and around the pan to create large soft curds. Continue this process, pausing for a few seconds in between to allow the curds to set. Cook the eggs until they are almost done, 8 to 10 minutes, then fold in the tomatoes. Cook for another 2 minutes, then turn off the heat and set the pan aside.

3. Pour half of the enchilada sauce into a 9 by 13-inch (23 by 33 cm) metal baking pan. Heat each tortilla over a gas flame or in a large skillet until softened. Working with one tortilla at a time, place a tortilla in the sauce and flip it to coat both sides with the sauce (a messy but important step). Place the coated tortilla on a plate, fill it with some scrambled eggs, and sprinkle with grated cheese. Wrap the tortilla and place it fold side down in the baking pan. Repeat with the remaining tortillas. Pour the remaining sauce on top of the enchiladas and sprinkle with the remaining cheese. Bake for about 15 minutes, until the cheese has melted. Serve with the guacamole, pico de gallo, and coconut yogurt alongside.

Tastes Like Grain Salad 2.0

One of the things I missed the most when I started my intuitive eating journey was grains—especially rice and quinoa. But I soon realized that properly cooked cauliflower rice can be the perfect replacement for any grain. So I began making and honing this recipe, which emulates grain salads perfectly. The best thing about this recipe is its versatility—it can be a main course for dinner, a side, or an excellent packed lunch for work, and it's great for large gatherings. It's filling and complements any protein. The dressing here is key. Don't skip it.

SERVES 4 TO 6

INGREDIENTS

1 large sweet potato (8 ounces/225 g), peeled and chopped

1 bunch Broccolini, trimmed

Olive oil, for drizzling

Kosher salt, or sub JF Spicy or JF Universal Salt

JF Cauliflower Rice (at right), cooked and cooled

2 Persian cucumbers, chopped

½ cup (55 g) chopped red onion

½ cup (75 g) crumbled vegan feta (I like Violife)

¼ cup (35 g) raw sunflower seeds

¾ cup (105 g) pomegranate seeds

½ cup (120 ml) Creamy Lemon, Garlic, and Dill Dressing (page 115), or to taste

For the JF Cauliflower Rice

2 tablespoons olive oil

1 clove garlic, minced

1 bag (24 ounces/680 g) frozen cauliflower rice

¼ teaspoon kosher salt or sub JF Spicy or JF Universal Salt, plus more to taste

Freshly cracked black pepper

PROCESS

1. Preheat the oven to 375°F (190°C). Line a 13 by 18-inch (33 by 46 cm) baking sheet with aluminum foil. Put the sweet potato on one half of the baking sheet and the Broccolini on the other half. Drizzle with olive oil, add a healthy sprinkle of salt, and roast until the Broccolini is charred and the sweet potatoes are tender, about 40 minutes.

2. While the sweet potatoes and Broccolini are in the oven, make the cauliflower rice: Put the olive oil and garlic in a large pan over medium-high heat and cook until the garlic begins to sizzle. Add the cauliflower rice and season with the salt and pepper. Mix using a spatula until the cauliflower rice is evenly coated in oil. Cook, stirring only every 3 to 4 minutes for a total of 12 to 15 minutes—you'll want to allow time for it to cook undisturbed so it develops crispy bits. Season with salt and let cool.

3. In a large bowl, combine the sweet potatoes, Broccolini, cauliflower rice, cucumbers, red onion, feta, sunflower seeds, and pomegranate seeds. Add your desired amount of dressing and toss thoroughly to coat. Leftover dressing will keep in an airtight container in the fridge for 1 week.

Deconstructed Spring Roll Salad

This is my new favorite way to eat as much color as possible. Made with simple kelp noodles (instead of rice noodles), romaine, butter lettuce, purple cabbage, basil, carrots, red pepper, Persian cucumbers, avocado, and a simple dressing of almond butter, coconut aminos, maple syrup, and apple cider vinegar. You can use any protein of your choice, but this goes especially well with sautéed wild shrimp. Wrap this up inside sheets of seaweed to enjoy a crunchy wrap instead of a salad. **SERVES 2 TO 4**

INGREDIENTS

For the kelp noodles

1 bag (1 pound/455 g) kelp noodles (save half of them in an airtight container for later)

1 teaspoon baking soda

Juice of 1 lemon (about 3 tablespoons)

3 cups (720 ml) hot water

For the sautéed shrimp

1 tablespoon lemongrass paste

1 pound (455 g) shrimp, preferably wild-caught, peeled and deveined

1 tablespoon olive oil

¼ teaspoon kosher salt, or sub JF Spicy Salt

Freshly cracked black pepper

For the dressing

⅓ cup (80 ml) almond butter

3 tablespoons coconut aminos

1 tablespoon maple syrup

2 tablespoons apple cider vinegar

Juice and zest of 2 limes (about ¼ cup /60 ml juice plus 2 teaspoon zest)

Sesame oil, for drizzling

Kosher salt, or sub JF Spicy Salt

For assembling the salad

1 head romaine, chopped

1 head butter lettuce, chopped

1 cup (95 g) shredded red cabbage

8 fresh basil leaves, thinly sliced

¼ cup (35 g) shredded carrot

¼ cup (35 g) chopped red bell pepper

2 small Persian cucumbers, chopped

1 avocado, peeled, pitted, and diced

Kosher salt, or sub JF Spicy Salt

2 tablespoons chopped fresh cilantro (optional)

2 nori sheets, for wrapping (I like Gimme's Avocado or Olive Oil sheets; optional)

PROCESS

Prepare the kelp noodles

1 Place the kelp noodles in a large bowl; add the baking soda and lemon juice. Pour the hot water over the top and mix well. Let soak for 10 minutes, or until tender; then drain. Set aside.

Sauté the shrimp

2 Put the lemongrass paste in a medium bowl. Add the shrimp, olive oil, salt, and pepper to taste and toss until the shrimp are evenly coated. Refrigerate for 15 minutes.

3 Heat a large skillet over medium heat. Add the shrimp with the marinade and cook for 1 to 2 minutes per side, then flip and cook for 1 more minute, or until opaque and cooked through. When the shrimp curl and just turn pink, remove them from the heat. Set aside to cool slightly before assembling the salad.

Make the dressing

4 In a small bowl, whisk together the almond butter, coconut aminos, maple syrup, apple cider vinegar, lime juice and zest, and a drizzle of sesame oil. Season with salt to taste.

Assemble the salad

5 Chop the shrimp into bite-size pieces. In a large bowl, combine the romaine, butter lettuce, red cabbage, basil, carrot, red pepper, cucumbers, avocado, kelp noodles, and shrimp. Add the almond butter dressing and toss to coat. Season with salt to taste and top with the chopped cilantro, if using.

"Eat Your Greens" Spicy Garlicky Broccoli Rabe Pasta

I love broccoli rabe, and it pairs nicely with pasta. This is an easy and delicious way to sneak some greens into your kids' diets. You can make this with regular pasta and cheese, but grain- and dairy-free alternatives work perfectly here too. Use elbow macaroni or fusilli to really get all the greens stuck inside the pasta. I personally love this dish for Sunday night dinners or when I'm craving something meat-free and filling. **SERVES 2 TO 4**

INGREDIENTS

1 bunch broccoli rabe, trimmed

⅛ teaspoon kosher salt, or sub JF Universal Salt, plus more for the cooking water

3 tablespoons olive oil

4 cloves garlic, minced

1 teaspoon crushed red pepper

Freshly cracked black pepper

1 box (8 ounces/225 g) grain-free pasta, cooked according to the package directions, ½ cup (120 ml) pasta water reserved

½ cup (50 g) freshly grated Parmesan cheese, plus more for serving

PROCESS

1 Fill a large pot with enough water to cover the broccoli rabe. Salt generously and bring to a boil. Meanwhile, fill a large bowl with water and ice; set aside. Add the broccoli rabe to the boiling water and boil until tender, about 6 minutes. Remove to the ice bath and let cool for about 2 minutes. Strain the broccoli rabe and squeeze as much water out of it as possible—you can wrap it with a clean dish towel or cheesecloth and then squeeze. Roughly chop the broccoli rabe.

2 Heat the olive oil in a large skillet over medium heat. Add the garlic and crushed red pepper and cook for about 1 minute, until fragrant, being careful not to burn the garlic. Add the broccoli rabe and season with the ⅛ teaspoon salt and a generous amount of freshly cracked black pepper. Sauté for 5 minutes, then add the reserved pasta water. Cook for 2 minutes, or until the water has slightly reduced, then add the cooked pasta; toss well to coat. Turn the heat to low, add the Parmesan, and toss to distribute. Serve with additional Parmesan and more freshly cracked black pepper.

Chicken Broccoli Bake

This is one of my earliest recipes that I posted right when I started my food Instagram account. My mother always used to make us lasagne when we were younger, so anything that feels like a casserole is home to me. I wanted to lighten it up a bit by using chicken instead of beef and played around with various vegetables until I landed on broccoli. It gives broccoli cheddar soup vibes. My favorite way to eat this is smothered in hot sauce. It is a lot of chicken, so feel free to put it in a wrap or serve it over a bed of simple salad or cauliflower rice. Like most casseroles, this is even better the next day. The plant-based ricotta gives it a rich creaminess without the grease of too much cheese. **SERVES 4 TO 6**

INGREDIENTS

- 1 small bunch broccoli (12 ounces/340 g), cut into small florets
- 1 teaspoon kosher salt, or sub JF Spicy or JF Universal Salt, plus more for sprinkling
- 3 boneless, skinless chicken breasts (6 to 8 ounces/170 to 225 g each)
- 2 cloves garlic
- 2 bay leaves
- 3 slices lemon
- 1 jalapeño chile, seeded and finely chopped
- 1 small red onion (4 ounces/115 g), chopped
- 1 teaspoon garlic powder
- ½ teaspoon freshly cracked black pepper, plus more to taste
- 6 ounces (170 g) mascarpone cheese or plant-based ricotta cheese, at room temperature (I like Kite Hill)
- 2 cups (230 g) shredded sharp cheddar cheese or plant-based cheddar cheese (I like Kite Hill)
- ½ cup (50 g) grated Parmesan cheese or plant-based Parmesan (I like Violife)
- Hot sauce, for serving

PROCESS

1 Preheat the oven to 400°F (205°C). Line a small baking sheet with parchment paper and spray with nonstick cooking spray. Spread out the broccoli florets on the sheet pan and sprinkle a generous pinch of salt on top. Bake the broccoli until crisp tender, 8 to 10 minutes. Set aside to cool. Reduce the oven temperature to 350°F (175°C).

2 Arrange the chicken breasts in a single layer in a 5-quart (5.7 liter) pot. Add the garlic, bay leaves, and lemon slices. Pour just enough room temperature water to cover the chicken by an inch (2.5 cm) or so. Bring to a boil over medium-high heat, then reduce the heat to low and simmer for 8 minutes, or until the chicken is fully cooked through. Using tongs, remove the chicken to a cutting board and allow to cool slightly.

3 Shred the chicken with a fork and transfer to a large bowl. Add the roasted broccoli, jalapeño, onion, garlic powder, salt, freshly cracked pepper, mascarpone, and 1½ cups (175 g) of the cheddar. Mix thoroughly using a fork. Spread the chicken mixture into a 10 inch/25 cm (2½-quart/2.4 liter) broiler-safe dish and top with the remaining ½ cup (55 g) cheddar and the Parmesan cheese. Bake for 22 minutes, then broil on high for about 3 minutes, until the top is browned and crispy. Let cool slightly, then cut it into portions and serve. Once cooled, store in the refrigerator for up to 2 days. Reheat portions on a plate in the microwave.

Spiced Roasted Carrots over a Sweet Potato Mash

This is a side that eats like a main, so it's perfect to serve to your vegan/vegetarian friends at dinner parties. It also makes the best holiday or easy dinner side. But don't reserve this for special occasions. The simple gremolata makes it feel much more formal and impressive for guests. It is so easy to throw together, and the best thing is, the ingredients are hearty shelf-stable veggies that should be found in your fridge on the regular, so you can make this on a whim at any time. **SERVES 4 TO 6**

INGREDIENTS

For the roasted carrots

- 1 teaspoon smoked paprika
- 1 teaspoon ground cumin
- ¼ teaspoon ground turmeric
- ¼ teaspoon ground ginger
- ⅛ teaspoon ground cinnamon
- ¼ teaspoon kosher salt, or JF Spicy Salt, plus more to taste
- 1 teaspoon olive oil
- 1 bunch large carrots (about 1 pound/455 g), trimmed and quartered lengthwise

For the mashed sweet potatoes

- 2 sweet potatoes (about 1½ pounds/680 g), peeled and cubed
- ½ teaspoon garlic powder
- 1 tablespoon olive oil
- 1 tablespoon plus ¼ teaspoon kosher salt, or sub JF Spicy Salt, plus more to taste
- 2 tablespoons butter or vegan butter, chilled (I like Monty's)

For the gremolata

- 1 cup (40 g) roughly chopped fresh cilantro, leaves and tender stems
- ½ cup (70 g) sunflower seeds, toasted, cooled, and roughly chopped
- Jalapeño chile, seeded and minced
- Zest of 2 limes
- Juice of 1 lime, plus more to taste
- 1 tablespoon olive oil
- Kosher salt, or sub JF Spicy Salt

For serving

- ½ cup (75 g) crumbled feta or vegan feta (I like Violife)
- ½ cup (90 g) thinly sliced red onion (preferably on a mandoline)
- 1 lime, for squeezing

(recipe continues)

Aunt Tinda's Pulled Pork

My aunt, like my mother, is a fantastic cook. I have distinct childhood memories of visiting her and my uncle Matt in their home in LA, where the kitchen always had something magical cooking. There would always be an amazing meal featuring some beautiful piece of cooked or braised meat. It was never too formal, but it was always a really interesting meal that felt different from my parents' way of cooking. They were experimental with their spice combinations. This recipe, which I made with my mother recently, is inspired by my aunt and uncle. It's simple and perfect—just like their style of cooking. Elevated but not fussy. **SERVES 6 TO 8**

INGREDIENTS

4 to 5 pound (1.8 to 2.3 kg) boneless pork shoulder blade roast (fresh pork butt), trimmed

2 tablespoons minced fresh oregano or dried oregano

2 tablespoons garlic powder

2 teaspoons ground cumin

1 tablespoon kosher salt, or sub JF Spicy or JF Universal Salt, plus more to taste

1 tablespoon freshly cracked black pepper, plus more to taste

¼ cup (60 ml) fresh lemon juice (about 2 large lemons)

¼ cup (60 ml) chicken broth, plus more as needed

1 medium yellow onion (6 ounces/ 170 g), thinly sliced

PROCESS

1 Preheat the oven to 350°F (175°C). In a small bowl, mix together the oregano, garlic powder, cumin, salt, and freshly cracked black pepper. Using a sharp knife, poke holes all over the pork and insert some of the spice rub into the holes using a small spoon (or work it in with your fingertips). Combine the rest of the spice rub with the lemon juice and rub all over the exterior of the pork.

2 Put the chicken broth and onion in a Dutch oven. Place the pork on top of the onions. Cover, place in the oven, and cook for 2½ to 3 hours. Check every hour to make sure it doesn't dry out. Add ¼ cup (60 ml) broth if it looks dry. Alternatively, if it looks too watery, uncover the pork for the last 20 minutes. Remove from the oven and let rest for at least 10 minutes. Pull off the meat using a fork or tongs (you can also slice or dice it). Taste and adjust the salt and pepper.

3 Serve as desired.

NOTE: *My favorite way to eat this is as tacos wrapped in small tortillas with toppings like California Guacamole (page 119), pickled onions, thinly sliced radish, cheese of your choice, fresh cilantro, plain coconut yogurt, and hot sauce.*

Smashed Potatoes

The elevated French fry—don't stress; take it out on your smashed potatoes. Serve these with anything or enjoy them as a main with your favorite salad for a perfect Meatless Monday option. Try these with sweet potatoes too. They're amazing. Don't skimp on the salt or the olive oil here; they make a big difference. No one likes an under-seasoned potato. **SERVES 2 TO 3**

INGREDIENTS

1 bag (approximately 1½ pounds/680 g) fingerlings and/or baby red or mini creamer potatoes, rinsed

2 tablespoons olive oil

⅛ teaspoon kosher salt, or sub JF Spicy, JF Universal, or JF Curry salt

⅛ teaspoon freshly cracked black pepper (medium to coarse ground)

For the toppings (optional):

1 recipe Chimichurri (page 116)

½ cup (75 g) crumbled feta cheese or vegan feta (I like Violife)

1 recipe Simple Tomato Sauce (page 118)

PROCESS

1 Fill a Dutch oven with water, salt generously, and bring to a boil. Add the potatoes to the boiling water and cook for 10 to 12 minutes, until tender when pierced with a fork. Rinse and drain. One by one, place the potatoes on a flat work surface. Using the palm of your hand, press down gently on each potato, just enough so the edges split. Don't completely flatten the potatoes or they will all fall apart in the pan. If the potatoes are too hot to touch, you can oil the bottom of a mug or glass and press down on the potatoes one at a time to smash.

2 In a large skillet, heat the olive oil over medium-high heat. Once the oil is hot, add the potatoes—you should hear a sizzle when they go into the pan. Sprinkle with the salt and pepper. Once golden-brown, flip the potatoes and repeat on the other side. Be careful not to burn them; you want crispy and charred potatoes, not blackened. Transfer to a wire rack set over parchment paper to absorb excess oil.

3 I love to top these with my Chimichurri Sauce; they are also amazing with crumbled feta and my Simple Tomato Sauce.

Bright Fennel Salad

This one makes me feel like I'm eating at a restaurant. It's more formal than my normal salads, which makes it great for dinner parties. I love fresh, crunchy salads with some citrus. The fennel pairs really nicely with Cara Cara oranges, but substitute whatever citrus you have on hand. Grapefruit makes the perfect alternative. Like Iggy Azalea, I sing "I'm so fancy" in my head every time I make this. **SERVES 2 TO 4**

INGREDIENTS

For the lemon vinaigrette

Juice of 1 lemon (about 3 tablespoons)

¼ cup (60 ml) olive oil

¼ cup (60 ml) honey

2 tablespoons Dijon mustard

Kosher salt, or sub JF Spicy Salt, and freshly cracked black pepper

For the salad

1 radicchio (8 ounces/225 g), chopped

½ medium fennel bulb (12 ounces/340 g), trimmed and thinly sliced

¼ cup (30 g) thinly sliced red onion

½ avocado, peeled, pitted, and diced

2 Cara Cara oranges, peeled and chopped

2 tablespoons sunflower seeds

Kosher salt, or sub JF Spicy Salt, and freshly cracked black pepper

PROCESS

Make the lemon vinaigrette

1 In a small bowl, whisk together the lemon juice, olive oil, honey, mustard, and salt and freshly cracked black pepper, until combined. Taste and adjust the seasoning as needed.

Assemble the salad

2 In a large bowl, combine the radicchio, fennel, and red onion with half the dressing. Massage lightly until the radicchio softens slightly. Add the avocado, oranges, sunflower seeds, and the remaining dressing and toss to coat. Season with salt and a generous amount of freshly cracked black pepper to taste.

Savory Pancakes (aka Grain-Free Blinis)

These grain-free blinis are perfect to top with whatever you feel like. My top pick is caviar. I've even hauled these to Paris so I could eat them at Caviar Kaspia with my friends (yup, true story). So don't be shy to haul them to any event where you might want to "have your caviar and eat it too." **MAKES ABOUT 35 BLINIS**

INGREDIENTS

5 large eggs

½ cup (120 ml) unsweetened almond milk, plus more as needed

1 cup (115 g) blanched almond flour

¼ cup (30 g) coconut flour

1 teaspoon baking powder

¼ cup (60 ml) avocado oil

¼ teaspoon kosher salt, or sub JF Spicy or JF Universal Salt, plus more for serving

For serving

1 cup (240 ml) crème fraîche or plain coconut yogurt

2 hard-boiled eggs, chopped

125 to 250 g caviar (I like Ossetra)

½ cup (20 g) chives, finely chopped

¼ cup (50 g) finely chopped red onion

¼ cup (40 g) capers

PROCESS

1 In a large bowl, whisk together the eggs, almond milk, almond flour, coconut flour, baking powder, avocado oil, and salt until smooth. The batter should be the consistency of a typical pancake batter. If it's too thick, add more milk. Make sure not to add too much, or the pancakes will be too wet.

2 In a large skillet over medium-low to medium heat, heat a thin layer of avocado oil. Drop 8 to 10 portions (about 2 teaspoons each) of batter onto the skillet. Cook until bubbles start to form, about 2 minutes. Flip and continue cooking until the second side is browned, about 1 minute. Transfer to a paper towel-lined plate. Repeat with the remaining batter. Top the blinis with crème fraîche, hard-boiled eggs, caviar, chives, red onion, and capers. Sprinkle with more salt, if desired, and serve.

New-Style Clean Stroganoff

This hearty dish is super comforting, so delicious, and so much lighter than the original I used to eat as a kid. The sliced mushrooms are amazing, but if you're not a fan, just omit them (Kevin isn't a mushroom guy, so instead of cooking them into the dish, I simply sauté some to serve on the side.) I've simplified this recipe by using ground beef over sliced, which I honestly personally prefer. The coconut yogurt makes this a little on the thinner side than traditional stroganoffs, but it does thicken over time. (Or see my suggested variation in the note below.) **SERVES 4 TO 6**

INGREDIENTS

1 tablespoon olive oil

8 ounces (225 g) sliced cremini or button mushrooms

½ cup (55 g) chopped yellow onion

1 pound (455 g) grass-fed ground beef

½ teaspoon kosher salt, or sub JF Spicy Salt, plus more to taste

2 tablespoons arrowroot flour

1 teaspoon paprika

2 teaspoons garlic powder

2 tablespoons coconut aminos (I like Coconut Secret Garlic Sauce & Marinade)

1 tablespoon freshly cracked black pepper, plus more for serving

4 cups (960 ml) beef broth (I like Kettle & Fire)

1 container (5 ounces/140 g) plain coconut yogurt (I like Culina or Cocojune)

1 box (8 ounces/225 g) grain-free fusilli

2 tablespoons unsalted vegan butter (I like Miyoko's)

¼ cup (13 g) chopped fresh flat-leaf parsley

PROCESS

1 Warm the olive oil in a large saucepan over medium heat. Add the mushrooms, turn the heat to medium-high, and cook until they begin to brown, 5 to 6 minutes. Add the onions and cook, stirring occasionally, until translucent, another 3 minutes. Add the ground beef and salt; break up the beef into chunks using a spatula and cook until browned, about 4 minutes. Add the arrowroot flour, paprika, garlic powder, coconut aminos, and freshly cracked black pepper and stir to combine.

2 Pour in the beef broth and bring to a boil. Reduce the heat to medium and let the sauce simmer until reduced, about 20 minutes. Turn down the heat to low and stir in the coconut yogurt to combine. Season with more salt and freshly cracked black pepper to taste.

3 While the sauce simmers, bring a large pot of salted water to a boil and cook the pasta according to the package instructions. Drain and add the butter to the cooked pasta, allowing the residual heat to melt it.

4 Serve the stroganoff over the pasta in individual bowls, topped with the parsley and more freshly cracked black pepper, if desired.

NOTE: *If you want to make a creamier version of this stroganoff, decrease the beef broth to 3 cups (720 ml), add 1 cup (240 ml) plain almond milk, and double the coconut yogurt to two 5-ounce (140 g) containers. If you are using grain-free pasta as I've instructed, be sure to store the leftover stroganoff and pasta in separate containers, as the grain-free pasta will disintegrate and turn the stroganoff mushy if they're combined.*

Grain- and Dairy-Free Bolognese Pasta Bake (aka "PMS Pasta Bake")

This is the ultimate Sunday comfort food or anytime you feel like you need something hearty and filling. It's beyond delicious served with my garlicky rabe, and the perfect thing to bake when you feel like something cozy and cheesy that mimics lasagne. Try not to eat the whole thing before you plate it! Everyone likes this. **SERVES 6 TO 8**

INGREDIENTS

2 boxes (8 ounces/225 g each) grain-free pasta (I like Jovial)

2 tablespoons olive oil

1 small yellow onion (4 ounces/115 g), finely chopped

3 cloves garlic, minced

1 tablespoon dried oregano

1 tablespoon dried basil

1½ pounds (680 g) grass-fed 80/20% ground beef

1 teaspoon crushed red pepper, plus more to taste

¼ teaspoon freshly cracked black pepper, plus more to taste

¼ teaspoon kosher salt, or sub JF Spicy Salt

3 cups (720 ml) Simple Tomato Sauce (page 118)

1 cup (110 g) shredded dairy-free mozzarella cheese (I like Violife)

½ cup (35 g) freshly grated dairy-free Parmesan cheese, plus more for topping if desired (I like Violife)

1 cup (245 g) dairy-free ricotta (I like Kite Hill)

1 recipe Garlicky Broccoli Rabe, chopped (from pasta recipe on page 198)

PROCESS

1 Preheat the oven to 350°F (175°C).

2 In a large pot of salted boiling water, cook your pasta according to the package instructions. Drain, reserving ⅓ cup (70 ml) pasta water. Rinse the pasta lightly to remove any starchy residue (when used in a saucy recipe, this type of grain-free pasta must be rinsed to prevent it from becoming gummy). Set aside while you make the sauce.

3 Heat the olive oil in a large saucepan over medium-high heat. Add the onion, garlic, oregano, and basil. Sauté until the onions are translucent, about 5 minutes. Add the ground beef, crushed red pepper, freshly cracked black pepper, and salt. Cook, stirring occasionally to break up the meat into smaller chunks, until the beef is browned almost all the way, about 5 minutes. Stir in the tomato sauce and heat until the sauce is bubbling, about 3 minutes. Lower the heat and cook, stirring often, until the sauce has reduced slightly, about 5 minutes. Add the pasta and stir to combine thoroughly.

4 In a small bowl, mix the mozzarella and Parmesan. Add a third of the pasta and Bolognese to a 9 by 13-inch (23 by 33 cm) baking dish, smoothing the pasta and sauce to create an even layer. Sprinkle with a third of the mozzarella and Parmesan mixture and add a few dollops of the ricotta. Add half of the remaining pasta and Bolognese and then half of the remaining cheese mixture and dollops of ricotta on top to create the second layer. Repeat the sequence with the last layer of pasta and Bolognese and then the cheeses. Shave additional Parmesan on top, if desired. Cover with aluminum foil and bake for 20 minutes, or until hot and bubbly. Cut into portions and spoon the JF garlicky broccoli rabe on top of the pasta when serving. This dish can also be made a day ahead and baked right before serving. Once cooled, store in the refrigerator for up to 2 days. Reheat portions on a plate in the microwave.

"I Wish I Were on Vacation in Cuba" Cuban Picadillo

Picadillo is one of my favorite fillings for empanadas. I'm a huge fan of the green olives and raisins that bring that perfectly salty-sweet combo to this dish. You can serve this warm over cauliflower rice or in a grain-free tortilla with plant-based cheese to create your own wrap. You can also pan-fry the tortilla to create a folded version that feels more like an empanada. But good luck getting that far—whenever I make this, I'm eating the meat directly out of a pan with a fork, and it barely makes it to the serving dish. I personally add extra olives to mine. Sweet and savory. List this as one of my favorite recipes. **SERVES 4 TO 6**

INGREDIENTS

- 2 tablespoons olive oil
- 2 medium yellow onions (6 ounces/170 g), chopped
- 4 cloves garlic, minced
- 2 pounds (910 g) ground beef
- 1 tablespoon ground cinnamon
- 2 teaspoons ground cumin
- 3 bay leaves
- ⅛ teaspoon ground cloves
- ⅛ teaspoon ground nutmeg
- 2 teaspoons kosher salt, or sub JF Spicy Salt, plus more to taste
- 1 can (28 ounces/795 g) fire-roasted tomatoes
- 2 tablespoons red wine vinegar
- ⅔ cup (95 g) raisins
- ⅔ cup (160 g) sliced green olives, such as Frescatrano or Castelvetrano

For serving

- 1 recipe JF Cauliflower Rice (page 194) or grain-free tortillas
- ½ cup (20 g) chopped fresh chives
- ½ cup (20 g) coarsely chopped fresh flat-leaf parsley
- Lime wedges, for squeezing

PROCESS

1 In a large pot over medium-high heat, heat the olive oil until it begins to shimmer. Add the onions and garlic and sauté for about 2 minutes. When they soften and become fragrant, add the ground beef. Using a spatula, break up the beef into large chunks. Cook, stirring occasionally, until the ground beef chunks begin to brown, about 5 minutes. Add the cinnamon, cumin, bay leaves, cloves, nutmeg, and salt and thoroughly combine. Turn down the heat to

medium and cook for about 1 minute, until the spices are fully incorporated. Stir in the tomatoes and vinegar. Lower the heat to medium-low, cover, and simmer for about 30 minutes to reduce.

2 Add the raisins and olives. Taste and adjust the seasoning. Cook, uncovered, until much of the moisture has evaporated, 12 to 15 minutes. Remove the bay leaves and serve warm over cauliflower rice or wrapped in a grain-free tortilla topped with chives, parsley, and a squeeze of lime.

"You Won't Miss the Potato" Cauliflower Latkes

I love latkes but never love the greasy, heavy feel of them. This cauliflower version was a happy accident for a holiday one year; it's shockingly satisfying and easy to make. Later, heavy latkes! These are where it's at. Top them with crème fraîche, sour cream or coconut yogurt, caviar and chives, or a chunky applesauce. You can also make them ahead of time, which makes them perfect for entertaining. People are always shocked at how good they are. Once you make these you'll never go back to potatoes. **MAKES 8 LATKES**

INGREDIENTS

2 tablespoons olive oil, plus more for frying

2 bags (10 ounces/280 g) frozen cauliflower rice

2 large eggs

1¼ teaspoons kosher salt, or sub JF Spicy or JF Universal Salt, plus more for sprinkling

⅓ cup (45 g) cornstarch or arrowroot flour

Toppings

½ cup (120 ml) crème fraîche, sour cream, or plain coconut yogurt

1.7 ounces (50 g) caviar (I like Ossetra)

2 tablespoons chopped fresh chives

½ cup applesauce, for a sweet version

PROCESS

1 Heat the olive oil in a large skillet over medium-high heat. Add the cauliflower rice and cook for 10 to 12 minutes, stirring occasionally, until the water from the cauliflower rice has evaporated and the grains have browned slightly. Remove from the heat and into a bowl; let cool completely.

2 In a large mixing bowl, whisk the eggs and salt. Add the cooled cauliflower rice and the cornstarch and mix to thoroughly combine. The batter should be thick and not runny.

3 Set a wire rack over a large baking sheet and line the wire rack with paper towels. Wipe the skillet with a paper towel to remove any bits of cauliflower rice. Heat over medium-high heat, then add just enough olive oil to cover the base of the pan. Working in batches of 2 to 4 at a time, add the cauliflower batter in 2-heaping-tablespoon (⅛ cup) portions and flatten with the back of a rubber spatula or measuring cup (do not crowd the pan). Fry until dark golden brown and crispy, 3 to 5 minutes, then flip and fry for 2 minutes more, or until browned. Remove the latkes to the paper towel-lined wire rack to drain. Sprinkle with more salt while still hot. Add more oil to the pan if needed and repeat the process with the remaining batter.

4 Serve the latkes with crème fraîche, sour cream or coconut yogurt, chives, and caviar; or applesauce for a sweet version.

Simple Slow-Cooker BBQ-Style Brisket

I never liked brisket till this. This is a great alternative to the classic brisket slathered in tomato sauce and French onion soup mix. I consider this a "holiday brisket," but I love making it pretty much all year round. Safe to say, this one is high up on the list of family favorites. Everyone asks for the recipe when I make it for holidays; it's that good because of its nod to BBQ rather than traditional, boring brisket. The leftovers are amazing chopped up and added to my Cauliflower Taco Rice (page 64) or stuffed into a cassava tortilla with melted cheese as a taco. My new thing is serving this brisket in tacos for Kol Nidre for "Friends Nidre" (not unlike "Friendsgiving"), on the eve of Yom Kippur, for a fun buffet instead of the traditional brisket buffet and sides. It works perfectly both ways, but I love making things more casual and delish wherever I can. Not to mention everyone loves tacos. **SERVES 6**

INGREDIENTS

2 tablespoons olive oil

1 fresh beef brisket (4 pounds/1.8 kg), well trimmed

2 teaspoons garlic powder

1 teaspoon onion powder

2 teaspoons paprika

3 teaspoons kosher salt, or sub JF Spicy or JF Universal Salt

1 teaspoon freshly cracked black pepper

½ teaspoon ground cumin

1 teaspoon chili powder

1 cup (240 ml) reduced-sugar barbecue sauce (I like Noble Made Less Sugar)

3 tablespoons minced garlic

2 tablespoons light brown sugar or brown coconut sugar

1 tablespoon Worcestershire sauce

1½ teaspoons cayenne pepper

(recipe continues)

PROCESS

1 Spray a slow cooker with nonstick olive oil or avocado oil spray and place the brisket inside the pot. Pour the 2 tablespoons olive oil over the brisket and use your hands to coat the meat. In a small bowl, mix together the garlic powder, onion powder, paprika, 2 teaspoons of the salt, the freshly cracked black pepper, cumin, and chili powder. Sprinkle half of the spice mix over one side of the brisket and rub it in well with your hands to coat. Flip the brisket and repeat on the other side. Turn the brisket fat side up.

2 In a small bowl, whisk together the barbecue sauce, garlic, light brown sugar, Worcestershire sauce, cayenne, and remaining 1 teaspoon salt. Using a pastry brush, spread half of the barbecue sauce on the fat side of the brisket (save the remaining barbecue sauce for broiling). Place the lid on the slow cooker and cook on high for 4 to 5 hours, until the brisket is tender.

3 Preheat the broiler on high. Line a large baking sheet with aluminum foil. Transfer the brisket from the slow cooker onto the lined baking sheet, fat side up (reserve the jus). Brush the remaining barbecue sauce on the brisket and broil until a crust begins to form, 8 to 10 minutes. Meanwhile, reduce the leftover liquid in the slow cooker on low for about 15 minutes. Pour the jus into a serving dish.

4 Remove the brisket from the broiler and let rest for 10 minutes prior to slicing. I like to use an electric knife when slicing my brisket; cut against the grain for perfectly thin slices. Serve the brisket alongside the jus.

"Don't Mess with the Whole Bird" Boneless Roasted Turkey Breast

This is a family favorite I make year-round. After having this, you may never buy deli turkey for sandwiches again. It is also perfect for a smaller Thanksgiving gathering, or if you are too scared to F with a whole bird. Making just the breast takes so much pressure off the cook! The last couple of years I have opted to make a few of these instead of a whole bird for our Thanksgiving dinners. Removing the stress of cooking a whole bird makes the day much easier to manage. Brine the breasts and prepare the compound butter beforehand, and the rest is just plug and play—success every time! I've even added 1 tablespoon chili powder and 2 teaspoons cumin to the compound butter for a Southwestern version.

SERVES 6 TO 8

INGREDIENTS

For the turkey brine

- ½ cup (110 g) packed light brown sugar or coconut sugar
- 8 fresh sage leaves
- 1 tablespoon kosher salt, or sub JF Spicy or JF Universal Salt
- 1 tablespoon black peppercorns
- 1 bunch fresh thyme (about 5 sprigs)
- 2 cloves garlic, smashed and peeled
- 2 skinless, boneless turkey-breast halves (about 2 pounds/910 g each)

For the butter rub

- ½ cup (1 stick/115 g) unsalted butter or vegan butter (I like Monty's brand), at room temperature
- 2 cloves garlic, finely minced
- 1 teaspoon chopped fresh or dried rosemary
- 1 teaspoon chopped fresh or dried thyme
- 2 teaspoons chopped fresh or dried parsley
- ½ teaspoon kosher salt, or sub JF Spicy or JF Universal Salt
- ¼ teaspoon freshly cracked black pepper

(recipe continues)

PROCESS

Brine the turkey

1. In a large container or bowl, combine the brown sugar, sage, salt, peppercorns, thyme, and garlic. Place the turkey breasts in the bowl and cover with cold or room temperature water, making sure the breasts are completely submerged. Cover the bowl and refrigerate for 12 hours or overnight.

Make the butter rub

2. Preheat the oven to 325°F (165°C). In a small bowl, mix together the softened butter, the garlic, rosemary, thyme, parsley, salt, and freshly cracked black pepper until well combined.

Roast the turkey

3. Remove the turkey breasts from the brine and discard all the soaking liquid. Pat the turkey completely dry and rub the herb butter all over the breasts. Place in a large shallow casserole or baking dish and roast for about 1 hour and 10 minutes. The turkey breasts are done when an instant-read thermometer inserted in the thickest part of the breast reaches 165°F (75°C). Remove from the oven and let rest for 15 minutes. Thinly slice the turkey and serve.

Grain- and Dairy-Free Stuffing

Stuffing is hands-down my favorite Thanksgiving side. Has been my entire life, and now I can eat it freely with all my holiday favorites—minus the grains and dairy. There is nothing better than having all the leftover sides the next day for lunch. I'll even eat this cold; it's that good. Serve it with my carrot and sweet potato mash (page 202), Grandma Lulie's Orange Cranberry Sauce (page 115), and Tastes Like Grain Salad 2.0 (page 194) to complete your holiday dinner. **SERVES 8**

INGREDIENTS

1 cup (2 sticks/240 ml) unsalted vegan butter (I like Monty's), plus more for brushing

2 grain-free sesame bread loaves (14 ounces/400 g each), cubed (I like Plantiful or AWG)

3 cups (330 g) chopped yellow onions

2 cups (200 g) chopped celery

6 cloves garlic, minced

1½ teaspoons kosher salt, or sub JF Spicy or JF Universal Salt

1 teaspoon freshly cracked black pepper

3 tablespoons finely chopped fresh sage

3 tablespoons finely chopped fresh rosemary

3 tablespoons finely chopped fresh thyme

3 tablespoons finely chopped fresh flat-leaf parsley

2½ cups (600 ml) chicken or vegetable broth

2 large eggs

PROCESS

1 Preheat the oven to 350°F (175°C). Brush a 9 by 13-inch (23 by 33 cm) casserole dish with butter; set aside. Line a large baking sheet with aluminum foil. Spread out the bread cubes on the baking sheet and toast for 15 minutes, or until crispy.

2 Melt the butter in a large skillet over medium heat. Stir in the onion, celery, garlic, salt, and freshly cracked black pepper. Cook, stirring constantly, until the vegetables are softened, about 8 minutes. Add the sage, rosemary, thyme, and parsley. After about 1 minute, add 1 cup (240 ml) of the broth. Taste and adjust the seasoning.

3 Transfer the toasted bread cubes to the buttered baking dish. Add the onion and celery mixture and toss well to evenly distribute. Let sit in the fridge for at least 2 hours or overnight.

4 When ready to bake: In a small bowl, whisk together the eggs and the remaining 1½ cups (360 ml) broth. Pour the egg mixture over the bread cubes. Bake for 45 to 50 minutes, until the egg mixture is set and the bread is golden. Serve immediately. Store cooled leftovers in an airtight container for up to 3 days.

Cauliflower Stuffing

This delivers a fall or Thanksgiving vibe year-round with any protein and is a perfect make-ahead dish. Or present it as a Thanksgiving side dish everyone will appreciate as a lighter option. Try leftovers of this stuffing inside a frittata for brunch over the holiday weekend. Your mother-in-law will love it. lol. **SERVES 4 TO 6**

INGREDIENTS

2 tablespoons olive oil (I like Kyoord)

1 tablespoon unsalted butter or vegan butter (I like Miyoko's)

1 clove garlic, chopped

1 medium yellow onion (6 ounces/170 g), chopped

2 stalks celery, chopped

2 carrots, peeled and chopped

1 bag (24 ounces/680 g) cauliflower rice (I like 365)

1½ teaspoons kosher salt, or sub JF Spicy or JF Universal Salt

¼ teaspoon freshly cracked black pepper

1 tablespoon unsalted butter or vegan butter (I like Miyoko's)

2 tablespoons finely chopped fresh rosemary

1 tablespoon finely chopped fresh sage

1 tablespoon chopped fresh thyme

¼ cup (13 g) chopped fresh flat-leaf parsley

½ cup (120 ml) chicken stock, plus more as needed

PROCESS

1. Heat the olive oil in a large skillet over medium heat. Add the garlic, onion, celery, and carrots and cook until tender, about 8 minutes. Add the cauliflower rice and cook for 8 to 10 minutes, stirring every few minutes, until browned. Season with the salt and freshly cracked black pepper

2. Add the butter, rosemary, sage, parsley, thyme, and chicken stock. Raise the heat to medium-high and cook for another 8 to 10 minutes, stirring every few minutes. Don't rush the cooking process here; allow the rice to slightly brown and crisp on the exterior. Remove from the heat and serve. Store cooled leftovers in an airtight container in the refrigerator for up to 2 days.

Friendsgiving Turkey Tacos with Pickled Onions

Instead of a turkey dinner, I served these turkey tacos at our first annual Friendsgiving a few years ago. And we've never gone back. In fact, on Thanksgiving I serve them as well, just for the kids. The adults can't resist sneaking in a few tacos here and there throughout the night. These make for the best build-your-own buffet bar situation for a large gathering. Serve with my Cauliflower Taco Rice (page 64). **SERVES 4 TO 6**

INGREDIENTS

For the pickled onions

1 small red onion (4 ounces/115 g), thinly sliced

Juice of 2 limes (about ¼ cup/60 ml)

¼ teaspoon kosher salt, or sub JF Spicy or JF Universal Salt

For the turkey tacos

1 tablespoon olive oil

1 small yellow onion (4 ounces/115 g), finely chopped

1 pound (455 g) ground turkey

2 cloves garlic, minced

1 teaspoon dried thyme

¼ teaspoon dried oregano

1 teaspoon kosher salt or sub JF Spicy Salt, plus more to taste

Freshly cracked black pepper

8 cassava, corn, or flour tortillas, charred

1 recipe California Guacamole (page 119)

1 recipe Pico de Gallo (page 121)

1 cup (120 g) shredded dairy or nondairy cheese of choice

½ cup (120 ml) sour cream or coconut yogurt (I like Cocojune)

Hot sauce of choice, for drizzling

Lime wedges, for squeezing

PROCESS

Make the pickled onions

1 In an airtight container, mix together the red onion, lime juice, and salt. Cover and refrigerate for at least 1 hour before serving.

Make the turkey tacos

2 Heat the olive oil in a large skillet over medium-high heat. Add the yellow onion and sauté until translucent, about 4 minutes. Add the ground turkey and garlic and sauté for about 3 minutes, breaking up the meat into small pieces with a spatula and allowing the meat to brown. Add the thyme, oregano, and salt and season with freshly cracked black pepper. Continue cooking, breaking up the meat into finer pieces, until browned throughout, about 2 minutes more. Taste and adjust the seasoning.

3 Serve the turkey on the charred tortillas. Top with the guacamole, pico de gallo, pickled onions, your choice of regular or dairy-free cheese, and sour cream or coconut yogurt. Drizzle with hot sauce and lime juice.

Anytime Gravy

I always thought you needed pan drippings to make gravy. Turns out that is not the case. Make this whenever you are in the mood for mashed potatoes or a gravy to pair with any protein. You literally can make this anytime. Save some, post-turkey, to dip your sandwich in.

SERVES 6

INGREDIENTS

- 4 tablespoons (½ stick/55 g) unsalted butter or vegan butter (I like Monty's)
- ½ cup (65 g) diced yellow onion
- 1 clove garlic, minced
- ⅛ teaspoon kosher salt, or sub JF Spicy or JF Universal Salt, plus more to taste
- 2 tablespoons all-purpose flour or blanched almond flour
- 1 cup (240 ml) chicken stock
- 1 tablespoon heavy cream or almond milk
- Freshly cracked black pepper
- 1 tablespoon arrowroot flour, if needed

PROCESS

1. Melt the butter in a medium saucepan over medium-high heat. Add the onion, garlic, and salt and sauté until the onions are browned, about 5 minutes. Whisk in the flour and then the chicken stock. Cook, whisking constantly, for about 30 seconds. Pour in the cream with one hand while whisking with the other. Continue cooking, whisking constantly, until the gravy thickens. Season with freshly cracked black pepper and more salt, if needed.
2. If the gravy is not thick enough, mix together the arrowroot flour and a little water in a small bowl. Slowly drizzle the slurry into the gravy and whisk to thicken and combine. Transfer the finished gravy to a blender and blend until smooth. Keep warm on the stovetop in a small saucepan until serving time. Store any leftovers in an airtight container in the refrigerator for up to 2 days.

Ropa Vieja with Coconut Cauliflower Rice

I sometimes have intense cravings for beef. And when I do, I prefer stewed and slow-cooked recipes that have some sort of sauce that can be eaten over rice. When I was growing up my mother would make a lot of pot roasts, and to me this recipe is an amped-up version of that with more flavor (don't get me wrong, I still love my mom's pot roast!). The coconut cauliflower rice becomes the perfect bed for the rich, stew-y beef. If you have extra time to spare, fry up some plantains to use as a topping and add some pepperoncini for a vinegary kick. Chop up leftover meat and add it to rice bowls for the kids for an easy main dish. **SERVES 4 TO 6**

INGREDIENTS

For the ropa vieja

- 2½ to 3 pounds (1.2 to 1.4 kg) flank steak
- Kosher salt, or sub JF Spicy Salt
- 1 teaspoon freshly cracked black pepper
- 2 tablespoons olive oil
- 1 yellow bell pepper, seeded and chopped
- 1 red bell pepper, seeded and chopped
- 1 large yellow onion (12 ounces/240 g), chopped
- 8 cloves garlic, minced
- 1 jalapeño chile, seeded and diced
- 2 bay leaves
- 3½ teaspoons sweet paprika
- 1 tablespoon dried oregano
- 2 teaspoons ground cumin
- ½ cup (120 ml) dry white wine
- 1 can (28 ounces/795 g) diced or crushed tomatoes

For the coconut milk cauliflower rice

- 1 tablespoon olive oil
- 1 small yellow onion (4 ounces/120 g)
- ½ teaspoon kosher salt, or sub JF Spicy Salt, plus more to taste
- 1 bag (24 ounces/680 g) frozen cauliflower rice
- ¾ cup (180 ml) full-fat unsweetened coconut milk

For serving

- 1 avocado, peeled, pitted, and sliced
- ½ cup (20 g) coarsely chopped fresh cilantro
- 1 red onion, thinly sliced
- ¼ cup (40 g) pepperoncini
- Hot sauce, for drizzling
- JF Spicy Salt, for sprinkling

(recipe continues)

PROCESS

Make the ropa vieja

1. Preheat the oven to 275°F (135°C). Pat the flank steak dry. Season both sides of the steak generously with the salt and freshly cracked black pepper. Heat a large oven-safe stainless steel or cast-iron skillet over medium-high heat. Once you see small wisps of smoke coming off the pan, add the olive oil. Add the steak to the pan and sear until one side is well browned, about 3 minutes. Flip and sear the other side of the steak for 1 to 2 minutes, until well browned. Transfer to a plate and set aside.

2. Turn down the heat to medium. Add the yellow and red bell peppers, the onion, garlic, jalapeño, and bay leaves to the pan. Sauté until the vegetables are tender, about 5 minutes. Season with the paprika, oregano, cumin, and salt to taste; mix thoroughly. Deglaze the pan with the wine and cook until the wine is reduced and the vegetables are softened, about 1 minute. Add the diced tomatoes and reduce for an additional 3 to 5 minutes, continuously scraping the bottom of the pan. Return the steak to the pan. Cover and bake for 2½ to 3 hours, until the meat is tender and shreddable.

3. Carefully transfer to a cutting board, but do not turn off the oven. Cut the steak against the grain into 3 large pieces. Return the pieces to the pan and shred them using two forks. Toss the meat to coat in the sauce. You can return the pan to the oven for about 5 minutes to reduce the sauce further if you'd like.

Make the coconut milk cauliflower rice

4. Heat the olive oil in a large skillet over medium-high heat. Add the onions and season with the salt. Cook, stirring often, until the onions are slightly browned, about 3 minutes. Add the cauliflower rice and salt. Sauté, stirring occasionally, until the rice is slightly crisp, about 8 minutes. Stir in the coconut milk. Let cook, stirring occasionally, until the coconut milk is absorbed and the cauliflower is slightly charred 6 to 8 minutes.

5. Serve the ropa vieja over the coconut-cauliflower rice, topped with the sliced avocado, cilantro, red onion, pepperoncini, hot sauce, and a sprinkle of salt.

You Won't Ever Make Mashed Potatoes Again

This Parmesan and garlic-mashed cauliflower is the perfect substitute for mashed potatoes. It's so good you'll find yourself making it in bulk and freezing a portion to use for meal prep later. The young and the old love these. The cream cheese and Parm give the mashed cauliflower a richness and flavor that feel just like potatoes. Yet again, one where you won't miss the taters. **SERVES 4 TO 6**

INGREDIENTS

2 medium heads (16 to 24 ounces/450 to 680 g) cauliflower, trimmed and roughly chopped

2 tablespoons olive oil

2 cloves garlic, minced

½ cup (50 g) freshly grated Parmesan cheese or plant-based Parmesan (I like Violife)

2½ tablespoons cream cheese or vegan cream cheese (I like Violife)

Kosher salt, or sub JF Spicy or JF Universal Salt, and freshly cracked black pepper

PROCESS

1 Place a steamer basket or colander in a large saucepan or stockpot. Add the cauliflower to the basket. Cover the bottom of the pot with an inch (2.5 cm) of water and bring to a boil. Reduce the heat to a simmer, cover, and steam the cauliflower until soft, about 10 minutes. Transfer to a food processor or blender and set aside.

2 Heat the olive oil in a small skillet over medium heat. Add the garlic and sauté for 2 minutes. Pour the garlic oil over the cauliflower in the food processor. Add the Parmesan and cream cheese, and season with salt and freshly cracked black pepper. Pulse the cauliflower mash until smooth (you can keep it on the chunkier side if you'd like). Taste and adjust the seasoning.

DESSERTS & BAKING

Cinnamon Swirl Bread

This is my version of a coffee cake. If you followed me during COVID, when we were all stuck at home, you know that this is a family favorite and is beyond easy. It also comes together in one bowl. You can make it with your kids as a fun first baking project to teach them the basics. It's also a crowd-pleaser and is a perfect sleepover thank-you present or a dinner party dessert. Try to make it last more than one day in the house—it's that good. Options for you below so that you can make the original or make it sugar-free and/or vegan. **MAKES ONE 9½ BY 5-INCH (24 BY 12 CM) LOAF OR 9 MUFFINS**

INGREDIENTS

For the cinnamon swirl

- 1 tablespoon ground cinnamon
- ⅓ cup (65 g) granulated sugar or coconut sugar
- ¼ cup (35 g) raisins (optional)
- ¼ cup (35 g) chopped toffee, such as Skor or Heath (optional)
- Assortment of nuts (optional)

For the glaze

- 2 tablespoons unsalted butter, ghee, or vegan butter, melted
- 1 cup (100 g) powdered sugar or 1 cup (215 g) date sugar (shown here; that's why it's darker)
- ½ teaspoon pure vanilla extract
- 2 tablespoons whole milk or almond milk

For the cake

- 1 large egg
- ⅓ cup (75 ml) avocado oil
- ¾ cup (150 g) granulated sugar or 1 cup (145 g) coconut sugar
- 1 cup (240 ml) whole milk or almond milk
- 2 cups (250 g) all-purpose flour
- 1 teaspoon baking powder
- ½ teaspoon kosher salt

Ground cinnamon and granulated or coconut sugar, for sprinkling (optional)

PROCESS

Make the cinnamon swirl

1 In a small bowl, mix together the cinnamon, sugar, raisins, if using, toffee, and nuts, if using. Set aside.

Make the glaze

2 In a medium bowl, combine the melted butter, powdered sugar, vanilla, and milk. Whisk until no sugar clumps remain. Set aside.

Make the cake

3 Preheat the oven to 350°F (175°C). Grease a 5 by 9½-inch (12 by 24 cm) loaf pan and line with parchment paper with a 2-inch (5 cm) overhang on opposite sides of the pan.

4 In a large bowl, whisk the egg, avocado oil, and sugar until the sugar has incorporated and the mixture turns pale yellow. Pour in the milk and whisk until fully incorporated. Add the flour, baking powder, and salt and whisk until no flour clumps remain—be sure not to over mix.

5 Pour a thin layer of batter on the bottom of the pan followed by a heavier layer of cinnamon sugar, then pour another thin layer of batter on top. Repeat until you have three alternating layers of cinnamon sugar and batter each, finishing with the cinnamon sugar swirl. Bake for 40 to 45 minutes. Poke the center of the bread with a toothpick—if it comes out clean, the cake is done.

6 Let the loaf cool completely in the pan on a wire rack, about 30 minutes. Remove from the pan and drizzle the icing over the top and sprinkle with cinnamon and sugar, if desired.

Lemon Poppy Seed Tea Cake

I have a soft spot for poppy seeds. This is reminiscent of one of my favorite muffins I would get at a bakery in Montecito when I was growing up, but now in loaf form. It's the most delicious tea cake and light lemony glaze. Light, but so satisfying and easy to freeze and save! This is perfect to take as a hostess gift for any brunch, or just to have in the house when you want something light and lemony with a cup of coffee or as a dessert. **SERVES 6 TO 8**

INGREDIENTS

For the icing

3 tablespoons fresh lemon juice (about 1 lemon)

1 cup (100 g) sifted powdered sugar or ½ cup (95 g) date sugar or coconut sugar (shown here; that's why it's darker)

For the cake

1½ cups (190 g) all-purpose flour or paleo flour (190 g), plus more for dusting (I like Bob's Red Mill)

¼ teaspoon baking powder

⅛ teaspoon baking soda

¼ cup (½ stick/55 g) unsalted butter, ghee, or vegan butter, softened at room temperature

½ cup (95 g) coconut sugar or date sugar

1 teaspoon fresh lemon zest

¾ cup (180 ml) 2% plain Greek yogurt or plain coconut yogurt, at room temperature

¾ teaspoon Madagascar vanilla

3 large eggs, at room temperature

2 tablespoons poppy seeds

PROCESS

Make the icing

1 In a medium bowl, whisk together the lemon juice and powdered sugar. Set aside.

Make the cake

2 Preheat the oven to 325°F (165°C). Line a 4¼ by 8½-inch (11 by 21.5 cm) loaf pan with parchment paper, leaving a 2-inch (5 cm) overhang on each side. Lightly spray with nonstick spray and dust with flour. Set aside.

3 In a small bowl, combine the flour, baking powder, and baking soda. Using a hand-held electric mixer on high, add the butter, sugar, and lemon zest to a large bowl and beat until creamy, about 3 minutes. Add the yogurt and vanilla and beat to combine. Add the eggs, one at a time, beating for 1 minute after each addition and scraping the bowl with a rubber spatula often. Add the dry ingredients into the bowl with the wet ingredients, beating on low until combined. Mix in the poppy seeds.

4 Pour the batter into the prepared loaf pan. Bake for 55 to 58 minutes, until a toothpick comes out clean. Cool the cake in the pan set on a wire rack for 10 minutes. Drizzle over the cake and allow the icing to set before lifting the cake out of the pan. Leftovers will keep in an airtight container for up to 4 days.

F*** the Flour Brownies

This is basically a cut-up flourless chocolate cake in brownie form, which makes for a less formal presentation that's also easier to make and execute. These brownies are fudgy, dense, and totally clean. Your kids won't care or even ask if they are gluten-, dairy-, and grain-free. Kevin loves these warmed up and topped with vanilla ice cream.

SERVES 9

INGREDIENTS

2 large eggs, at room temperature

½ cup (95 g) coconut sugar

¼ cup (60 ml) maple syrup

⅓ cup (75 ml) coconut oil, melted

1 teaspoon pure vanilla extract

¾ cup (85 g) blanched almond flour

⅔ cup (65 g) unsweetened cocoa powder

¼ teaspoon baking soda

¼ teaspoon sea salt

For the chocolate drizzle (optional)

1 teaspoon coconut oil

¼ cup (45 g) semisweet chocolate chips (I like Guittard coconut-sugar chips)

PROCESS

Make the brownies

1 Preheat the oven to 350°F (175°C). Line an 8-inch (20 cm) square baking dish with parchment paper, leaving a 2-inch (5 cm) overhang on opposite sides.

2 In a large bowl, whisk the eggs, coconut sugar, maple syrup, melted coconut oil, and vanilla extract until combined. In a medium bowl, mix the almond flour, cocoa powder, baking soda, and sea salt. Slowly incorporate the dry ingredients into the wet ingredients, stirring with a rubber spatula to incorporate. Pour the batter into the lined baking dish. Bake until a tester inserted in the middle comes out clean, 15 to 18 minutes. Set the pan on a wire rack to cool completely. Grab the parchment overhang to remove the brownie from the pan. If not serving right away (unlikely!), store in an airtight container for up to 3 days.

If making the chocolate drizzle

3 In a microwave-safe bowl, heat the chocolate chips and coconut oil in 10-second intervals until melted, stirring to combine. Cool slightly and drizzle over the brownies. Slice into servings and enjoy.

Grain-Free "No Corn" Cornbread

I love this recipe because you would never guess this "cornbread" doesn't actually have corn in it. I limit corn because of its sugar content, but no worries here, since it's corn free! It's the perfect snack or side dish when you're in the mood for something savory. Serve it alone, smothered in vegan butter, or with one of my soups or chilis. You can thank me later for this gem. It also works well toasted as a vessel for my brisket (page 224) or whenever you need a soft sandwich bun. Try serving my Clean Joes (page 142) as minis, using this un-cornbread as the bun; it's such a good combo. **SERVES 9**

INGREDIENTS

- 3 large eggs, at room temperature
- ⅓ cup (75 g) unsalted butter or vegan butter, melted and cooled (I like Miyoko's or Monty's)
- ½ cup (120 ml) full-fat coconut milk
- 2 teaspoons fresh lemon juice
- ¼ cup (60 ml) raw honey
- ½ cup (95 g) coconut sugar
- 1¾ cups (175 g) blanched almond flour
- ¼ cup (30 g) arrowroot flour
- 2 tablespoons (20 g) coconut flour
- 1½ teaspoons baking powder
- ½ teaspoon baking soda
- ½ teaspoon kosher salt, or sub JF Spicy Salt

PROCESS

1. Preheat the oven to 325°F (165°C). Line an 8-inch (20 cm) baking pan with parchment paper, leaving a 2-inch (5 cm) overhang on opposite sides.

2. In a large bowl, whisk together the eggs, butter, coconut milk, lemon juice, honey, and coconut sugar. In a medium bowl, mix the almond flour, arrowroot flour, coconut flour, baking powder, baking soda, and salt. Add the dry ingredients to the bowl with the wet ingredients. Using a rubber spatula, mix to incorporate. Transfer the batter to the pan and bake until golden and a tester inserted in the middle comes out clean, 32 to 34 minutes. Let the bread cool completely in the pan before slicing. Store leftovers in an airtight container for up to 3 days.

Grain-Free Lemon Olive Oil Cake

Cakes like these are my preferred choice for dessert, as I can't handle cloyingly sweet desserts filled with too much sugar. I made this when I was craving a light, lemony cake. This is one that turned out better than I expected and is totally clean. I've included the option of a chocolate drizzle on top for extra sweetness. But you can omit the drizzle for a more universal cake and serve with macerated berries instead or alone with coffee for breakfast. The touch of almond flavor is what makes this one of my favorites. **SERVES 8**

INGREDIENTS

For the cake

2 cups (230 g) blanched almond flour
1 teaspoon baking powder
¼ cup (35 g) tapioca flour
½ teaspoon kosher salt
½ teaspoon cream of tartar
4 large eggs, yolks and whites separated
¾ cup (145 g) coconut sugar
Zest of 1 lemon (about 1 tablespoon)
¼ cup (60 ml) fresh lemon juice
½ cup (120 ml) olive oil
1 teaspoon pure vanilla extract
½ teaspoon almond extract
½ teaspoon cream of tartar

For the chocolate drizzle

⅓ cup (85 g) semisweet chocolate chips (I like Guittard coconut-sugar chips)
1 teaspoon refined coconut oil

PROCESS

Make the cake

1. Preheat the oven to 325°F (165°C). Lightly spray an 8-inch (20 cm) round springform pan with olive or avocado oil. Line the bottom with a parchment paper round and spray again.

2. In a medium bowl, combine the almond flour, baking powder, tapioca flour, and salt. Whisk the dry ingredients well to break up any clumps of almond flour. Set aside.

3. In a large bowl, whisk together the egg yolks, ½ cup (95 g) of the coconut sugar, and the lemon zest until smooth. Add the lemon juice, olive oil, vanilla extract, and almond extract; whisk to combine. Add the dry ingredients from the medium bowl to the wet ingredients. Thoroughly mix using a rubber spatula, ensuring no dry clumps remain.

4 In a separate large bowl, using a handheld mixer on high, whisk the egg whites and cream of tartar until foamy, about 2 minutes. With the mixer running, add the remaining ¼ cup (50 g) coconut sugar, a few teaspoons at a time, until stiff peaks form, about 5 minutes. Fold a third of the egg whites into the batter and mix until no white streaks remain, then fold in the remaining egg whites and mix to combine.

5 Pour the batter into the prepared springform pan. Smooth the top using an offset spatula or the back of a spoon. Bake until the top of the cake is golden brown and a tester inserted into the center comes out clean, 40 to 42 minutes. Transfer the pan to a wire rack and let the cake cool before unmolding. The cake can be made a day ahead, then drizzled with the chocolate before serving.

Make the chocolate drizzle (if using)

6 In a microwave-safe bowl, melt the chocolate chips and coconut oil in a microwave in 10-second intervals until smooth, stirring with a spatula between each interval. Drizzle over the top of the cooled cake using a spoon. Allow to set for 5 minutes before slicing.

Double-Chocolate Brownie Cookies

These are essentially the love child of a brownie and a cookie. Honestly, they're not the most glamorous-looking cookies, but if I'm in the mood for something salty and sweet, these cookies offer the perfect combination. Extra-spicy salt on top makes these sweet and savory. Don't overbake them: They are better chewy! I love dunking them into almond milk late-night while standing in my kitchen.

MAKES 12 COOKIES

INGREDIENTS

2 large eggs, at room temperature

2 teaspoons Madagascar vanilla extract

1 teaspoon refined coconut oil, melted

½ cup (125 g) coconut sugar

1 cup (255 g) raw almond butter

⅓ cup (30 g) unsweetened cocoa powder

½ teaspoon baking soda

¼ teaspoon kosher salt

⅓ cup (60 g) semisweet chocolate chips (I like Guittard coconut-sugar chips)

PROCESS

1 Preheat the oven to 350°F (175°C). Line two baking sheets with parchment paper.

2 In a large bowl, whisk the eggs, vanilla, coconut oil, and coconut sugar until the sugar has melted. Add the almond butter and whisk until fully incorporated and no clumps of almond butter remain. Add the cocoa powder, baking soda, salt, and chocolate chips. Stir using a rubber spatula until the mixture develops a dough-like texture.

3 Roll the cookie dough into 12 balls and place them on the prepared baking sheets about 2 inches (5 cm) apart. Sprinkle the cookies with additional salt and bake for 8 to 10 minutes, until set and crackly on top. Let the cookies cool on the baking sheet until just cool enough to handle but still warm before you serve them. The cookies will keep in an airtight container at room temperature for up to 5 days.

Mom's Da Bomb Banana Bread

This is my most requested recipe (I even have college kids DM me for the recipe or send me pics of themselves when they make it). This recipe is a family heirloom I got from my mother (love you, Mom). I keep the original printout of the recipe from the old cookbook she used as good luck in my kitchen. It's a classic banana bread that makes use of those desperate bananas sadly withering away in some corner of your fruit basket. Bring some cinnamon, butter, and chocolate chips to the party, and who can resist the retro charm of this evergreen classic? Bring this to work or to friends' homes for events. Do it clean or live it up and enjoy the OG version. Trust me, they won't stop talking about it. **MAKES ONE 9½ BY 5-INCH (24 BY 12 CM) LOAF, 12 MUFFINS, OR 3 MINI LOAVES**

INGREDIENTS

4 tablespoons (½ stick/55 g) unsalted butter, ghee, or vegan butter, softened at room temperature

1 cup (200 g) granulated sugar or 1 cup (190 g) coconut sugar

1 large egg, at room temperature

½ teaspoon pure vanilla extract (I like Beyond Good)

3 large overripe bananas, gently mashed with a fork

1½ cups (190 g) all-purpose flour, or 1¾ cups (200 g) blanched almond flour plus ½ cup (70 g) tapioca flour

1 teaspoon kosher salt

1 teaspoon baking soda

½ teaspoon ground cinnamon

¾ cup (140 g) chocolate chips (I like Guittard coconut-sugar chips)

⅓ cup (40 g) semisweet chocolate chips (I like Guittard coconut-sweetened chips)

½ cup (50 to 80 g) nuts of choice (optional)

PROCESS

1. Preheat the oven to 325°F (165°C). Grease and line a 5 by 9½-inch (12 by 24 cm) loaf pan with parchment paper with a 2-inch (5 cm) overhang on each end.

2. Using a handheld or stand mixer fitted with a paddle or whisk, mix the butter and sugar on medium speed until smooth and creamy, 1 to 2 minutes. Add the egg and vanilla and mix until the consistency is even. Gently mix the mashed banana into the egg mixture. Be sure not to break up the banana too much; it's nice to have chunks throughout the bread.

3. In a medium bowl, whisk the flour, salt, baking soda, and cinnamon until well combined. Slowly add the dry mixture into the wet mixture. Using a rubber spatula, mix just until no dry clumps remain—don't overmix. Add the chocolate chips, dark chocolate chunks, and nuts, if using, and mix until evenly dispersed.

(recipe continues)

4 Pour into the prepared loaf pan. Bake for 45 to 55 minutes, checking with a toothpick after 45 minutes if you used all-purpose flour; the bread is done if the toothpick comes out completely clean. If using almond flour plus tapioca flour, bake for 55 to 60 minutes and check with a toothpick at the 55-minute mark.

5 Allow the loaf to cool completely in the pan set on a wire rack, about 30 minutes. Leftover banana bread wrapped in plastic wrap will last about 5 days at room temperature.

Gluten-Free, Dairy-Free Cheesecake

Cheesecake is one of my favorite desserts. This recipe has no dairy or grain but all the creaminess and satisfaction of the "real thing." It's also a great foundation for any flavor add-ons or accoutrements of your choice. The caramel sauce from my Not-Too-Sweet Seven-Layer Bars (page 262) is a delicious topping for this if you want it extra sweet. Or you can simply top it with macerated berries or caramelized bananas and a quick chocolate drizzle. Also, it's pretty impressive-looking dressed with fruit or the topping of your choice. People will be shocked it's dairy-free and made of cashews. It travels really well and keeps in the fridge, so you can make it ahead and not have to stress. The crust on this is insane and feels exactly like the original. I like to top mine with fresh berries and mint. **SERVES 8**

INGREDIENTS

For the filling

- 1 cup (5 ounces/120 g) raw cashews
- 1 cup (240 ml) full-fat unsweetened coconut milk
- 8 ounces (225 g) dairy-free cream cheese (I like Violife)
- ¼ cup (50 g) date sugar
- 1 teaspoon pure vanilla extract
- 1 tablespoon maple syrup
- ⅛ teaspoon kosher salt

For the crust

- 14.25-ounce (405 g) box grain-free graham crackers (12 cookies or 7.5 ounces equals 1½ cups crumbs) (I like Sixteen Mill Honey Cinnamon Sweet Thins)
- ¼ cup (30 g) blanched almond flour
- 3 tablespoons coconut oil, melted
- 2 tablespoons maple syrup

(recipe continues)

PROCESS

1 Preheat the oven to 350°F (175°C). Grease an 8-inch (20 cm) springform pan with nonstick spray. Line the bottom with parchment paper and spray with more nonstick spray.

Make the filling

2 In a small saucepan, combine the cashews with just enough water to cover the nuts. Bring to a boil, then reduce the heat to low. Simmer until the cashews are tender, about 8 minutes. Turn off the heat and let sit while you prepare the crust.

Make the crust

3 Using a food processor, pulse together the graham crackers and almond flour into fine crumbs. Add the coconut oil and maple syrup. Pulse to combine. Transfer the crumb mixture to the springform pan and press the crumbs firmly and evenly into the pan using the back of a measuring spoon to line the bottom of the pan. Bake the crust for 12 minutes, or until golden.

Finish the filling

4 Drain the soaked cashews and transfer to a blender. Add the coconut milk, cream cheese, date sugar, vanilla, maple syrup, and salt. Blend well until very smooth. Pour the filling over the crust.

5 Bake for 40 to 42 minutes, until just firm. Transfer to a wire rack to cool completely, then chill in the fridge for at least 4 hours, until set.

FISHER

Not-Too-Sweet Seven-Layer Bars

I love a seven-layer bar, so I wanted to create my own version that's a bit cleaner than the classic. These are sticky, sweet, coconutty, and chocolatey—all the things that cure my PMS symptoms. The key here is making sure the caramel is the right consistency so the bars hold their shape. Practice really does make perfect with this one. Cut them into long sticks for an impressive presentation. **MAKES 12 SMALL BARS**

INGREDIENTS

For the crust

1½ cups (175 g) blanched almond flour

2½ tablespoons maple syrup

⅓ cup (75 ml) refined coconut oil, melted

For the caramel

¼ cup (60 ml) refined coconut oil, melted

¼ cup (60 ml) maple syrup

2 tablespoons unsweetened creamy almond butter

¼ teaspoon pure vanilla extract

Pinch kosher salt

For the sweetened coconut condensed milk

1 cup (240 ml) unsweetened full-fat coconut milk

¼ cup (60 ml) maple syrup

For the toppings

¾ cup (130 g) semisweet chocolate chips (I like Guittard coconut-sugar chips)

Unsweetened coconut flakes, for sprinkling

A few pinches ground cinnamon

PROCESS

1 Preheat the oven to 350°F (175°C). Line an 8-inch (20 cm) square baking pan with parchment paper.

Make the crust

2 Mix together the almond flour, maple syrup, and coconut oil in a medium bowl until combined. Press the mixture evenly into the bottom of the baking pan and bake for 14 minutes, or until golden.

Make the caramel

3 While the crust is baking, in a small saucepan over low heat, whisk together the coconut oil, maple syrup, almond butter, vanilla extract, and salt. Keep whisking until the mixture completely dissolves and the caramel has thickened slightly, about 5 minutes. Remove from the heat and set aside.

Make the sweetened coconut condensed milk and assemble

4 In another small saucepan over medium heat, whisk together the coconut milk and maple syrup and bring to a boil. Reduce the heat to low and simmer for about 5 minutes, until the mixture has thickened slightly. Remove from the heat and set aside.

5 When the crust is done, sprinkle the unsweetened coconut flakes over the top. Lightly press half the chocolate chips into the crust and spread the caramel sauce on top. Pour the sweetened condensed milk evenly on top and bake for about 20 minutes.

6 Remove the pan from the oven and sprinkle the remaining chocolate chips, extra coconut flakes, if desired, and the cinnamon on top. Let cool completely, then transfer the pan to the freezer for about 30 minutes to harden. Cut the bars into squares to serve. Leftovers can be stored in an airtight container for about 4 days.

Paleo Chocolate Chip-Almond Butter Cookies

These taste like a coconut macaroon, almond butter, and a chocolate chip cookie had a baby. People love these suckers. Make sure not to overbake them or they will be dry AF. **SERVES 12**

INGREDIENTS

1 cup (115 g) almond flour

¼ cup (35 g) coconut flour

1 teaspoon baking soda

1 teaspoon kosher salt

6 tablespoons (95 g) almond butter

¾ cup (145 g) coconut sugar

6 tablespoons (90 ml) refined coconut oil

1½ teaspoons pure vanilla extract

1 large egg

1 cup (175 g) semisweet chocolate chips (I like Guittard coconut-sugar chips)

PROCESS

1 Preheat the oven to 350°F (175°C). Grease a large cookie sheet with nonstick coconut oil spray or line the pan with parchment paper.

2 In a large bowl, whisk together the almond flour, coconut flour, baking soda, and salt. In another large bowl, combine the almond butter, coconut sugar, coconut oil, and pure vanilla extract. Using a hand mixer, mix together the wet ingredients. Once combined, beat in the egg. Slowly mix in the dry ingredients. Using a rubber spatula, roughly mix in the chocolate chips. Refrigerate for at least 1 hour, but longer, up to 3 hours, if you can.

3 Drop the batter by tablespoons onto the prepared pan. Bake for 7 to 8 minutes, until the batter is set and the tops are starting to turn golden brown. Remove the cookies to a wire rack to cool. Store in an airtight container for up to 4 days.

Paleo Banana Cake with Chocolate Ganache Frosting

Baked goods are one of the hardest things to dupe (in my opinion) while eating grain- and gluten-free. This super-simple homemade paleo banana cake with chocolate ganache on top hits right every time, and before you know it, you'll have a grain-free, gluten-free, dairy-free, and garbage-free dessert ready. The beauty of this cake is that it's not supposed to look perfect or professional—just freestyle the ganache and dig right into the whole thing with a fork. Add 1 cup (175 g) dark chocolate chips to make it extra delish. Take this to an office birthday party and everyone will freak out. **MAKES ONE 8-INCH (20 CM) SQUARE CAKE**

INGREDIENTS

For the cake

- 3 ripe bananas, peeled
- 3 large eggs, at room temperature
- 1½ teaspoons pure vanilla extract
- 3 tablespoons maple syrup
- 2½ cups (290 g) blanched almond flour
- ½ cup (65 g) arrowroot flour
- 1 teaspoon baking soda
- ½ teaspoon baking powder
- ¼ teaspoon kosher salt

For the ganache

- 1½ cups (255 g) bittersweet chocolate chips (I like Guittard coconut-sugar chips)
- ½ cup (120 ml) unsweetened almond milk or nut milk of your choice, plus a few extra teaspoons if needed

PROCESS

Make the cake

1. Preheat the oven to 350°F (175°C). Line an 8-inch (20 cm) square baking pan with parchment paper overhanging by 2 inches (5 cm) on opposite sides of the pan.
2. In a food processor, pulse the bananas, eggs, vanilla, and maple syrup until smooth. Add the almond flour, arrowroot flour, baking soda, baking powder, and salt; pulse to combine.
3. Pour the batter into the prepared pan. Bake for 30 to 35 minutes, until the cake is golden brown on top and a tester or toothpick inserted into the middle comes out clean with just a few crumbs. Set on a wire rack to cool completely. Remove from the pan.

Make the ganache

4 Put the chocolate chips and nut milk in a small bowl. Microwave in 10-second intervals until melted—be careful not to scorch the chocolate. If needed, add a few more teaspoons milk and stir until the melted chocolate is shiny and spreadable. Spread the ganache on the cooled cake with a spatula. Place the cake in the fridge for 15 minutes to set the ganache before cutting. Leftovers can be stored on a cake stand or in another airtight container for up to 3 days.

Grain-Free Biscotti

It was killing me not being able to dunk a biscotti into my coffee post-dinner or while on vacation. So I made one. Here is my clean version of the classic biscotti, perfect with a cup of coffee/tea or completely on its own. If you know me, you know I actually do take these to work or on trips with me so I can have a couple to dunk in my coffee and not feel left out. They store and travel really well. The longer they sit the harder they get, so it's a bonus if they get stale and crunch more like the classic. Play around finding your favorite add-ins, whether that's nuts, dried fruit, and/or chocolate. My personal favorite is just chocolate chips. **MAKES 16 LONG BISCOTTI**

INGREDIENTS

- 2 large eggs, at room temperature
- ½ cup (1 stick/115 g) unsalted butter or vegan butter, melted and cooled
- ½ cup (120 ml) honey or ¾ cup (145 g) coconut sugar
- 1 teaspoon almond extract
- 1 teaspoon kosher salt
- 3½ cups (405 g) blanched almond flour
- 1 teaspoon baking soda
- 1 teaspoon ground cinnamon
- ½ cup (65 g) unsalted shelled pistachios, coarsely chopped
- ½ cup (85 g) semisweet chocolate chips
- ⅓ cup (45 g) cranberries or raisins

PROCESS

1. Preheat the oven to 325°F (165°C). Line two large baking sheets with parchment paper.
2. In a large bowl, whisk together the eggs, butter, honey, almond extract, and salt. Add the almond flour, baking soda, and cinnamon and, using a rubber spatula, mix to incorporate. Fold in the pistachios, chocolate chips, and cranberries. Chill the dough in the refrigerator for 20 minutes (the dough is quite sticky, and chilling helps it become more manageable).
3. Using a rubber spatula, scoop out half the dough onto each of the prepared baking sheets. Using your hands, form the dough halves into loaves approximately 8 by 2-inches (20 by 5 cm). Bake for 30 minutes. Remove from the oven and cool for at least 15 minutes, until the loaves are just warm.

4 Slice the loaves on a diagonal into 1-inch-thick (2.5 cm) pieces using a serrated knife, cleaning the knife with a paper towel between cuts. Be gentle—they're still delicate at this stage. Place the biscotti cut side down on the baking sheet. Return to the oven for 1 hour to 1 hour 15 minutes, until the biscotti are completely dry and crisp. Begin checking at 55 minutes to see how much moisture is still left on the cookies. If the cookies are still moist at 75 minutes, reduce the oven temperature to 270°F (130°C) and continue baking until the biscotti are completely dried.

Grain-Free Chocolate Biscotti

These might be my favorite baked good in the book. They work day to night, keep well, and are the perfect cookie to dunk in anything at any time. AND they are better after a few days of sitting on your cake stand, so they last longer (that is if you don't eat them all). Perfect for potlucks and office parties, too. **MAKES 16 LONG BISCOTTI**

INGREDIENTS

2 large eggs, at room temperature

½ cup (1 stick/115 g) unsalted butter or vegan butter, melted and cooled

1¼ cups (240 g) coconut sugar

2 teaspoons pure vanilla extract

1 teaspoon kosher salt

3½ cups (405 g) blanched almond flour

1 teaspoon baking soda

3 tablespoons unsweetened cocoa powder

1 tablespoon ground cinnamon (optional)

½ cup (85 g) semisweet chocolate chunks (I like Hu Kitchen)

PROCESS

1 Preheat the oven to 325°F (165°C). Line two large baking sheets with parchment paper.

2 In a large bowl, whisk the eggs, butter, coconut sugar, vanilla extract, and salt until combined. Add the almond flour, baking soda, cocoa powder, and cinnamon, if using, and, using a rubber spatula, mix to incorporate. Fold in the chocolate chunks. Chill the dough for 20 minutes (the dough is quite sticky, and chilling helps it become more manageable).

3 Using a rubber spatula, scoop out half the dough onto each of the prepared baking sheets. Using your hands, form the dough halves into loaves approximately 8 by 2 inches (20 by 5 cm). Bake for 30 minutes. Remove from the oven and let cool for at least 15 minutes, until the loaves are just warm.

4 Slice the loaves on a diagonal into 1-inch-thick (2.5 cm) pieces using a serrated knife, cleaning the knife with a paper towel between cuts. Be gentle—they're still delicate at this stage. Place the biscotti cut side down on the baking sheet. Return to the oven and bake for 1 hour to 1 hour 15 minutes, until the biscotti are completely dry and crisp. Begin checking at 55 minutes to see how much moisture is still left on the cookies. If the cookies are still moist at 75 minutes, reduce the oven temperature to 270°F (130°C) and continue baking until the biscotti are completely dried.

Seed Bread, Simple and Everything

This is one of my early-on recipes when I started to eat grain free. All of the bread options were too flat for me, and I sometimes craved more toasted seeds than actual toast. The result is sort of mind-blowing and it comes together very fast with this simple recipe. The loaves keep very well in the fridge in an airtight container for about a week, but they can also be sliced and frozen so you can pull a slice out at a moment's notice when you are craving it. As with all the recipes, feel free to make this one your own by swapping in different seeds or adding raisins or dried fruit. I think it's great to have a plain and an everything version of this bread on hand, depending on your mood. Make one loaf at a time, slice, freeze, and experiment! **MAKES 2 LOAVES**

INGREDIENTS

For the Universal Seed Bread

1 cup (140 g) raw sunflower seeds

½ cup (130 g) pumpkin seeds

½ cup (50 g) sliced almonds

⅓ cup (55 g) black chia seeds

⅓ cup (50 g) hemp hearts

2 tablespoons white sesame seeds

⅓ cup (55 g) flaxseeds

½ cup (60 g) psyllium husk powder

1½ teaspoons kosher salt, or sub JF Universal Salt

½ teaspoon coconut sugar

1½ cups (360 ml) boiling water

For the Everything Seasoned Seed Bread

2 tablespoons poppy seeds

2 tablespoons onion powder or (preferably) granulated onion

2 tablespoons garlic powder or (preferably) granulated garlic

1 cup (140 g) raw sunflower seeds

½ cup (130 g) pumpkin seeds

½ cup (50 g) sliced almonds

⅓ cup (55 g) chia seeds

⅓ cup (50 g) hemp hearts

2 tablespoons white sesame seeds

⅓ cup (55 g) flaxseeds

½ cup (60 g) psyllium husk powder

1½ teaspoons kosher salt

1¾ cups (420 ml) boiling water

(recipe continues)

PROCESS

Make the Universal Seed Bread

1 Preheat the oven to 400°F (205°C). Grease a 4½ by 8½-inch (11 by 21.5 cm) loaf pan really well.

2 In a large bowl, combine the sunflower seeds, pumpkin seeds, almonds, chia seeds, hemp hearts, sesame seeds, flaxseeds, psyllium husk powder, salt, and coconut sugar. Pour the boiling water over the seed mixture. Mix well using a rubber spatula and form into a uniform dough.

3 Push the dough into the loaf pan and bake for 1 hour. Let cool completely (about 1 hour) in the loaf pan. Turn the bread out onto a cutting board to slice.

Make the Everything Seasoned Seed Bread

1 Preheat the oven to 400°F. Grease a 5 by 9-inch (12 by 23 cm) loaf pan really well.

2 In a large bowl, combine the poppy seeds, onion powder, garlic powder, sunflower seeds, pumpkin seeds, sliced almonds, chia seeds, hemp hearts, sesame seeds, flaxseeds, psyllium husk powder, and salt. Pour the boiling water over the seed mixture. Mix well using a rubber spatula and form into a uniform dough.

3 Push the dough into the loaf pan. Bake for 1 hour. Let cool completely (about 1 hour) in the loaf pan. Turn the bread out onto a cutting board to slice.

Storage

4 I like to keep mine in an airtight container in the fridge for up to a week (if it lasts that long!). Or you can slice it into individual slices and freeze it. Thaw slices at room temperature. Once thawed, toast in the toaster.

ACKNOWLEDGMENTS

It's hard to believe that the little girl in after-school cooking class would one day go on to create her own cookbook. Over the years, I carefully collected recipes and meticulously placed them into binders, often modifying them along the way to make them my own. The thought of putting my recipes together for a cookbook never crossed my mind. Here we are, and I'm so grateful for all the support along the way.

Thank you to my "food community"; your passion and positive reinforcement in my DMs truly provided the "push" I needed—not only to choose to create this cookbook but also to support me through the process of making it. Your messages of encouragement, personal stories, and inquiries truly gave me the strength to do this. You guys are the best xx.

Thank you, **ABRAMS BOOKS**, for taking a chance on me and allowing me to share such a big part of my life with the world.

HOLLY DOLCE, my editor, thank you for believing in me. I'll never forget our first Zoom, when your face literally popped up and, with a huge smile, said, "I know how to make this book." I knew at that moment you were the one. Your positive energy and bright tone have always kept me moving to get this right in my own voice, with no writer except for your help. You speak JF, and I adore you forever. Thank you.

EVE ATTERMAN, my agent, you believed in me from the start and helped me build the most incredible team to bring this book to life. You understood the warmth, edge, and tone needed for every aspect of the book, and you nailed it all. It's just who you are. There were no stupid questions, and for that, I'm so grateful. You never felt like an agent; you were always a kind and supportive friend who gave the right advice when needed and got the job done—a perfect balance.

QUENTIN BACON, my dream photographer. Perfect natural light, zero ego, and the kindest collaborator on the planet. I never dreamed I would ever have Ina Garten's photographer shooting my first cookbook, but here we are, and I'm already excited for the next one. Your calm presence, chill playlist, and precise expertise in lighting made for fast shoot days that never ran over and kept us all on time. (Quentin also has an amazing line of all-natural beeswax skin care products—the lip balm is my personal fave.)

CHLOE ANDRAE, thank you for being an integral part of the team. Your eye was incredibly helpful choosing favorite shots along the way.

DEB WOOD, my designer/art director and "partner in crime," constantly texting on weekends about colors and fonts. You are a creative force, and I'm so thankful to have had you by my side to help execute my vision. You, my friend, are a true visionary, and I adore you more than I can say.

FRANCES BOSWELL, legendary food stylist, I'll admit I was intimidated at first, given the work you have done with famous chefs and prestigious publications. You were so cool and inspiring. Collaborating with you to transform and elevate my simple recipes was incredible. Thank you for your eye, splatters, balance, and beautiful execution on this project.

CYNTHIA GASPARRE, your prep, sourcing, organization, and cooking were so valuable throughout the shoot. You were so kind, had such a chill vibe, and made sure everything ran smoothly in the kitchen on set. I still miss our ritual of crossing off completed recipes with your special black pen as the days progressed.

MAEVE SHERIDAN, the queen of props with the most positive, powerful light in the room. I'll never be able to source a perfect plate, glass, or fork without you. I still hear you saying, "Ooh, wait, I have this; let me run and grab it," and you did, and it was always just right. You are a master of the art of home goods and textures.

ANIKAH SHAOKAT, your input and adjustments were spot on. Thank you for confirming that all the recipes can now be replicated easily and precisely.

JULIA BODNER, my manager, thank you for betting on me. I'm excited for the future.

NINA STUART RUDIKOFF, my ride-or-die publicist for over seven years and my biggest cheerleader, you were with me from the very beginning of this wild food adventure. Whether it was getting recipes on the website, helping with the selects for this book, or correcting my grammar, you played an important part in this journey. The "No Corn" Cornbread and Tastes Like Grain Salad are for you, girl. Also, shout-out to **COURTNEY BURKE**, your assistant and my other PR "police" of many years—you always came in with a new clean-food recommendation or raved about a recipe. Your support over the years at JF means more than you know.

NATASHA NATHAN, my best friend for thirty years and the one who introduced me to Kevin, you are my biggest beacon of strength and positive reinforcement at any hour of the day. You know me inside and out and always encourage me with your signature "Come the fuck on, Jen, you got this." Your unconditional support and tough love the past three decades mean everything to me. Thank you and love you.

SARAH MCFADDEN, my oldest friend in the world, from the age three in Santa Barbara, California. Our calls throughout the years and this entire process were incredibly helpful and meaningful. You are my original chosen family, and I love you.

To "**THE 4 TRIBECA TROTTERS**," my ride or die neighborhood crew, thank you for dealing with me constantly changing my orders and asking "the oil" questions at NYC restaurants while drinking and dining out, letting me use you as my "taste testers" over the years (your significant others included), and listening to me as I talked about wanting to make this book and then listening to me more as I actually made it. I love you guys more than life.

RACHEL MOSKOWITZ, my first friend in Kevin's NYC crew and my "Frister" for life, no one makes me laugh more than you with your dry and fast humor. You are always there for me unconditionally.

LAURAN WALK, my neighbor of ten years and best source of quiet, calm, yet fierce guidance. You are a pillar of strength and trusted support.

CORTNEE GLASSER, my first text of the day about fashion or to correct my typos and grammar on Instagram, you are thoughtful, funny, and compassionate and share my sunglasses obsession.

AYESHA HAIDER, you keep us out the latest, and you are always up for the fun. You are strong on so many levels, smart, global, and always honest.

CHARLIE WALK, thank you for being a great mentor over the years and my biggest "hype man." Your guidance and advice have been invaluable. I appreciate you being you.

SHADI MULLIN, you are the one person in my life who loves a health food store more than I do. You get the food and follow the food (with even more discipline than I do), and, more importantly, you get me. Thank you for always listening. Love you.

My mother, **LAUREN MULLINS**, thank you for your love, support, and warmth in teaching me how to cook. Watching you in the kitchen preparing meals for all of us over the years was the best guiding light. Also, thank you for choosing to send me to Montessori school, where I learned to cook an egg. Oh, and for your banana bread recipe, which is now famous in the "community." You truly are da bomb, and the best mom a girl could ask for. I love you.

To my brothers, **TODD** and **MARC**, who have been there since the beginning of my food journey, at all the family BBQs with Pops, the food prep with Mom, and listening to Dad tell us to "be self-starters, do the dishes." I love you guys.

REGGIE, my mother-in-law, thank you for always calling to share a positive story you heard from a friend about my food. Those phone calls over the years meant more than you know. I love you.

To my immediate and extended family, thank you for all your kind texts, DMs, and phone calls about my food; they have been incredibly meaningful throughout my journey. I love you all.

My kids, **SHANE** and **DREW**, thank you for being so patient with me while I share our kitchen and your food with the world. I know it's not easy to have almost every meal photographed and documented, but you played a meaningful role in this cookbook, and I couldn't have done it without you. I'm so grateful that you have opened your minds and hearts to my cooking; if it weren't for you, so many of these recipes would not exist, let alone this book. You are my everything, I love you.

KEVIN, you are the reason this book and my entire life have happened. You are not only the best husband and life partner but also the best and most positive, hot food tester a girl could ask for. You let me fly, listen intently, and have next-level patience. Oh, and thank you for the daily coffee in bed; you are my rock and king. I love you.

INDEX

D

E

F

R

S

Editor: Holly Dolce
Designer: Deb Wood
Design Manager: Heesang Lee
Managing Editor: Lisa Silverman
Production Manager: Denise LaCongo

Library of Congress Control Number: 2025931670

ISBN: 978-1-4197-7814-8
eISBN: 979-8-88707-471-9

Printed and bound in China
10 9 8 7 6 5 4 3 2 1

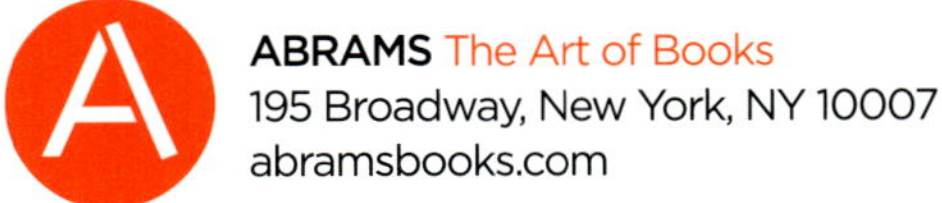

ABRAMS is represented in the UK and Europe by Abrams & Chronicle Books, 1 West Smithfield, London EC1A 9JU and Média-Participations, 57 rue Gaston Tessier, 75166 Paris, France.
www.abramsandchronicle.co.uk and www.media-participations.com
info@abramsandchronicle.co.uk